SAY IT IN
CHINESE
(Mandarin)

SAY IT IN
CHINESE
(Mandarin)

by
Dr. Nancy Duke Lay

Instructor of Chinese at the
New School for Social Research, N.Y.,
and Assistant Professor of English
as a Second Language at
City College of New York

DOVER PUBLICATIONS, INC.
New York

The Dover *Say It* series is prepared under the editorial supervision of Nancy D. Gross.

Published in Canada by General Publishing Company, Ltd., 30 Lesmill Road, Don Mills, Toronto, Ontario.
Published in the United Kingdom by Constable and Company, Ltd., 10 Orange Street, London WC2H 7EG.

Say It in Chinese (*Mandarin*) is a new work, first published by Dover Publications, Inc., in 1980.

International Standard Book Number: 0-486-23325-1
Library of Congress Catalog Card Number: 73-94347

Manufactured in the United States of America
Dover Publications, Inc.
180 Varick Street
New York, N.Y. 10014

In memory of my father
JOSEPH DUKE S. LAY
黎鐸成
1893–1972

CONTENTS

CONTENTS

INTRODUCTION

Say It in Chinese (Mandarin) is based on the official language of the People's Republic of China and the Republic of China (Taiwan). Called *pŭ-tūng-hwà* (language of the common people) or *gwó-yŭ* (national language), it is derived from a north Mandarin dialect originally spoken in the area around Peking.

There are over one billion speakers of Chinese. Chinese is really a broad term that encompasses a number of related regional dialects with varying degrees of mutual intelligibility. In its different dialects, Chinese is the native language of 94% of the population of the People's Republic and Taiwan. It is also the mother tongue of substantial ethnic Chinese communities scattered across Southeast Asia, Singapore, Malaysia, Indonesia, the Philippines and the United States.

Three quarters of the world's Chinese speakers regard Mandarin as their main language. Most speakers of other Chinese dialects can understand and communicate in Mandarin to some extent. Thus, Mandarin Chinese can reach more people than any other single language in the world.

Written Chinese employs ideographic characters, which are individual symbols that have come to be associated with a single concept but give no sure idea of pronunciation. Therefore, monolingual speakers of different Chinese dialects may not be able to communicate orally with a great deal of success, but all literate people can read, write and understand the same characters.

Since the establishment of the People's Republic of China on the mainland in 1949, one of the Peking government's top priorities has been the standardization and propagation of a single national language based on

Mandarin. Vocabulary has undergone some change to bring the language in line with ideology, complex characters have been simplified and a totally new system of romanization has been developed (see Table, p. xviii).

This book is designed to be of the widest possible use wherever Mandarin is spoken and understood.

NOTES ON THE USE OF THIS BOOK

This book is divided into sections according to the various topics and situations encountered by the traveler. It is not the purpose of this book to explain the points of Chinese grammar. But it is useful to remember that word order in Chinese is extremely important and you would do well to stay close to the form of the sentences and substitutions provided.

While most sections of this book are alphabetized according to the English phrases, the sections on Chinese food specialties are alphabetized according to the transcribed Chinese names. This has been done in order to familiarize you with typical dishes and facilitate ordering in restaurants.

The material in this book has been selected chiefly to teach you many essential phrases, sentences and questions for travel. It will serve as a direct and interesting introduction to the spoken language if you are beginning your study. The sentences will be useful to you whether or not you go on to further study. With the aid of a dictionary, many sentence patterns included here will answer innumerable needs, for example: "She has lost [her handbag]." The brackets indicate that substitutions can be made for these words with the use of a bilingual dictionary. In other sentences, for the words in square brackets you can substitute the words immediately following (in the same sentence or in the indented entries below it). For example, the entry

Turn [left][right] at the next corner.

provides two sentences: "Turn left at the next corner" and "Turn right at the next corner." Three sentences are provided by the entry

> Give me a seat [on the aisle].
> —by a window.
> —by the emergency exit.

As your Chinese vocabulary grows, you will find that you can express an increasingly wide range of thoughts by the proper substitution of words in these model sentences.

Please note that whereas brackets always indicate the possibility of substitutions, parentheses have been used to indicate synonyms or alternative usage for an entry, such as:

> Hello (OR: How are you?).

In this case, the alternative usage is preceded by (OR:).

Occasionally, parentheses are used to clarify a word or to explain some nuance of meaning that may be implicit or understood in either the English or the Chinese phrase. The abbreviation "(LIT.)" is used whenever a literal translation of a Chinese phrase or sentence is supplied.

You will notice that the word "please" has been omitted from many of the English sentences. This was done merely to make them shorter and clearer, and to avoid repetition. To be polite, however, you should use the equivalent for "please," *ch'ing*, at the beginning of the Chinese phrase.

The written Chinese characters for each phrase have been included for those who may wish to use them for reference or further study. They also provide an additional tool for making yourself understood, since the desired phrase may be pointed out to a Chinese speaker to clarify your spoken Chinese if necessary.

You will find the extensive index at the end of the book especially helpful. Capitalized items in the index refer to section headings and give the number of the page on which the section begins. All other numbers refer to *entry numbers*.

All the entries in the book are numbered consecutively. With the aid of the index, you will find many words and phrases at a glance.

PRONUNCIATION

We have supplied an explanatory chart of the transcription used in this book to aid you in correct pronunciation. Read over the notes carefully so you may become familiar with the transcription system. There are three different transcription systems for Chinese which are considered standard (see Table, p. xviii for details). We have adopted the Yale system of romanization for this book. This system employs the least number of special and unfamiliar symbols, while at the same time providing an accurate guide to Chinese pronunciation and tone which both the beginner and the more advanced student can follow with little difficulty.

Pay close attention to the explanation of the sounds of Chinese, the transcription of each phrase, and the tone markings for each Chinese word. Since any transcription system can serve at best only as an approximation of correct pronunciation, the more conscientiously you follow the transcription the better your chances of getting your ideas across. You will discover that there are probably no sounds in Chinese that you cannot pronounce with a little practice and, using this book as a tool, you will be surprised at how well you will be able to make yourself understood.

CONSONANTS

Remarks

b   pronounced as *b* in *b*ad but with no vibration of vocal cords.

ch   pronounced as *ch* in *ch*op but with tip of tongue against lower front teeth.

d   pronounced as *d* in *d*eaf but with no vibration of vocal cords.

dz   pronounced as *ds* in ki*ds*.

f   pronounced as *f* in *f*an.

g   pronounced as *g* in *g*ap but with no vibration of vocal cords.

h   pronounced as *h* in *h*ot but with much stronger puff of air.

j   pronounced as *j* in *j*ust but with tip of tongue against lower front teeth and no vibration of vocal cords.

k   pronounced as *k* in *k*it but with stronger puff of air.

l   pronounced as *l* in *l*et.

m   pronounced as *m* in *m*et.

n   pronounced as *n* in *n*ot.

ng   pronounced as *ng* in si*ng*er, not as in fi*ng*er.

p   pronounced as *p* in *p*in but with stronger puff of air.

r   at the beginning of a syllable or alone pronounced as French *je* or *z* in English a*z*ure; elsewhere as *ir* in sh*ir*t.

s   pronounced as *s* in *s*it.

Tran-
scription   *Remarks*

sh   pronounced as *sh* in *sh*ip but with back of tongue touching roof of mouth.

sy   pronounced as *sh* in *sh*eep but with tip of tongue against lower front teeth and no rounding of lips.

t   pronounced as *t* in *t*ap but with stronger puff of air.

ts   pronounced as *ts* in ki*ts*.

w   pronounced as *w* in *w*et.

y   pronounced as *y* in *y*es.

yw   pronounced as *y* in *y*es and *w* in *w*et simultaneously, with tongue in position to form *y* but lips rounded to form *w*.

VOWELS

a   between *w* and *ng*, pronounced *o* as in *l*o*ng*; between *yw* and *n*, as *a* in b*a*t; between *y* and *n*, as *a* in h*a*nd; elsewhere as *a* in f*a*ther.

ai   pronounced as *ai* in *ai*sle.

au   pronounced as *au* in s*au*erkraut.

e   at the end of a syllable and immediately preceded by *sy*, *y*, or *yw*, pronounced as *e* in m*e*t; elsewhere as *u* in h*u*t or c*u*ff.

ei   pronounced as *ei* in w*ei*gh.

i   at the end of a syllable, pronounced as *ee* in b*ee*; elsewhere as *i* in b*i*t.

o   pronounced as a sound halfway between *u* in f*u*r and *oa* in *oa*r.

ou   pronounced as *ou* in d*ou*gh.

Tran- scription	Remarks
u	immediately preceded by *sy* or *y*, pronounced as a combination of *oo* in sh*oo*t and *ee* in b*ee*; in the middle of a syllable and immediately preceded by any sound other than *sy* or *y*, pronounced as *oo* in t*oo*k; at the end of a syllable and immediately preceded by any sound other than *sy* or *y*, pronounced as *oo* in h*oo*t.
r	pronounced as *ur* in c*ur*, or *ir* as in sh*ir*t.
z	pronounced as *oo* in b*oo*k but keeping the lips tense, not rounded.

TONES

Chinese is a tone language. Any Chinese syllable spoken in isolation has one of four basic tones or no tone at all (referred to as neutral tone). Very often, two or more monosyllables are composed of the same sounds and the only factors which indicate differences in meaning are the different tones.

The tones of Chinese are indicated and produced in the following manner:

First tone	ā	a high, level tone which starts near the highest pitch of the speaker's voice and continues unchanged; *jyā* "home."
Second tone	á	a high, rising tone which starts at the middle of the speaker's range and quickly rises to the highest pitch; *jyá* "lined."
Third tone	ǎ	a low, rising tone which starts below the middle range of the speaker, reaching the lowest pitch and then rising up to above middle range; *jyǎ* "artificial."
Fourth tone	à	a high, falling tone which starts near the highest part of the speaker's range and falls quickly towards the lowest pitch; *jyà* "vacation."
Neutral tone	a	a short, middle pitch pronounced quickly with no emphasis; the *de* in *wǒ de* "my."

The tones vary in duration. The third tone is held the longest, while the first and second tones are longer in comparison to the fourth tone. The neutral tone is extremely short and barely sustained.

In normal, rapid speech, Chinese speakers do not always give the full or true tones to each monosyllable. Often only the word on which the logical emphasis and stress lie is pronounced with its full tone. Our transcription automatically indicates these major changes in tone, so you do not have to memorize the complex patterns of tone alteration.

COMPARATIVE TABLE OF TRANSCRIPTIONS OF CHINESE SOUNDS

This book employs the Yale system of romanization. The table below lists equivalent spellings in *pīn yīn* and Wade-Giles. *Pīn yīn*, declared the official system of the People's Republic in 1958, is used in elementary school education, government documents, romanized publications and signs, and geographical and proper names. *Pīn yīn* is gradually being adopted by Western media, scholars and language teachers. Wade-Giles was developed by two British scholars and was widely used in the late 19th and early 20th centuries. It fell into disuse in the mid-20th century, although it is still found occasionally in transcribing names of places, dynasties and historical personages in books, newspapers and magazines.

YALE (*this book*)	PEKING (*Pīn yīn*)	WADE-GILES
a	a	a
ai	ai	ai
au	ao	ao
b	b	p
ch	ch, q	ch'
d	d	t
dz	z	ts, tz
e	e	e, ê, eh
ei	ei	ei
er	er	êrh
f	f	f
g	g	k
h	h	h
i, r, y, yi, z	i, yi	i, ih, ǔ

YALE (*this book*)	PEKING (*Pīn yīn*)	WADE- GILES
j	j, zh	ch
k	k	k'
l	l	l
m	m	m
n	n	n
ng	ng	ng
o	o	o
ou	ou	ou
p	p	p'
r	r	j
s	s	s, ss
sh	sh	sh
sy	x	hs
t	t	t'
ts	c	ts', tz'
u	u	u
ung	ong	ung
wa	ua, wa	ua, wa
wai	uai, wai	uai, wai
we	ue	wê
wei	uei, ui, wei	uei, ui, wei
wo	uo, wo	uo, wo, o
ya	ia, ya	ia, ya
yau	iao, yao	iao, yao
ye	ie, ye	ie, ieh, ye
you	iou, iu, you	iu, yu
yu, yw	ü	ü
ywe	üe, yue	üe, üeh

SAY IT IN
CHINESE
(Mandarin)

EVERYDAY PHRASES

1. Hello (OR: **How are you?**).
nín hău?　您 好 ?

2. Good day. r̀-ān.　日 安.

3. Good morning. dzău-ān.　早 安.

4. Good afternoon. wŭ-ān.　午 安.

5. Good evening. wăn-ān.　晚 安.

6. Good night (LIT.: **See you tomorrow**).
míng-tyān-jyàn.　明 天 見.

7. Welcome. hwān-yíng.　歡 迎.

8. Goodbye (LIT.: **See you again**).
dzài-jyàn.　再 見.

9. See you later (**au revoir**).
hwéi-tóu-jyàn.　回 頭 見.

10. Yes.* dwèi-le (OR: shŕ).　對 了 (是).

11. No.* bú-dwèi (OR: bù-syíng).　不 對 (不 行).

12. Perhaps (OR: **Maybe**). hwò-jě.　或 者.

13. Please. chǐng.　請.

14. Allow me. ràng wŏ.　讓 我.

15. Thanks. syè-syè.　謝 謝.

* An affirmative answer is generally expressed by repeating the
main verb of the interrogative sentence. A negative answer can
usually be expressed by repeating the question verb, preceded by
bù.

16. You are welcome (OR: **Don't mention it**).
bú-syè.   不 謝.

17. All right (OR: **Very good**).
hén-hǎu.   很 好.

18. It doesn't matter.   méi-gwān-syi.   沒 關 係.

19. Don't bother.   yùng-bu-jáu.   用 不 着.

20. I am sorry (OR: **Excuse me**).
dwèi-bu-chǐ.   對 不 起.

21. You have been very kind.
nín tài hǎu le.   您 太 好 了.

22. You have been a great help.
chéng nín bāng-máng.   承 您 幫 忙.

23. Come in.   chǐng jìn.   請 進.

24. Come here.   lái jèr.   來 這 兒.

25. Come with me.   gēn wǒ lái.   跟 我 來.

26. Come back later.
děng yí-syà hwéi-lái.   等 一 下 回 來.

27. Come early.   dzǎu lái.   早 來.

28. Wait a minute.   děng-yi-děng.   等 一 等.

29. Wait for us.   děng wǒ-men.   等 我 們.

30. Not yet.
hái méi-yǒu (OR: hái wèi dìng).   還 沒 有 (還 未

31. Not now.   bú-shì syàn-dzài.   不 是 現 在.

32. Listen!   tīng!   聽 !

33. Look out (OR: **Watch out**)! jù-yì!   注 意 !

34. Be careful.   syǎu-syīn.   小 心.

SOCIAL PHRASES

35. May I introduce (LIT.: **This is**) [**Mrs. Wang**].
jèi shì [wáng tài-tai].   這是 [王太太].

36. —Miss Li. —lǐ syáu-jye.   —李小姐.

37. —Mr. Jwang.
—jwāng syān-sheng.   —莊先生.

38. —Comrade Chyan.*
—chyán túng-jr̀.   —錢同志.

39. I am glad to meet you.
wǒ hěn gāu-syìng de jyàn dàu nín.   我很高興的見到您.

40. How are you (OR: **How do you do**)?
nín hǎu?   您好?

41. Very well, thanks, how about you?
hén hǎu. syè-syè. nǐ ne?   很好. 謝謝. 你呢?

42. How are things (LIT.: **Is everything all right**)?
yí-chyè dōu hǎu ba?   一切都好吧?

43. So, so.
mǎ ma hū hu (OR: wú-swǒ-wèi).   馬馬虎虎 (無所為).

44. What's new?
yǒu shém-ma syīn de?   有什麼新的?

45. Won't you sit down?
chǐng dzwò.   請坐.

46. Congratulations. gūng-syǐ.   恭喜.

47. All the best. wàn shì rú-yì.   萬事如意.

48. Happy birthday. shēng-r̀ kwài-lè!   生日快樂.

* The word "comrade" in the People's Republic is the preferred form of address for waiters, porters, cab drivers and other people involved in service.

49. I like you very much.
wǒ hěn syǐ-hwān nín. 我很喜歡您.

50. I love you. wǒ ài nǐ. 我愛你.

51. I'd like to see you again.
wǒ syǎng dzài lái jyàn nǐ! 我想再來見你!

52. Let's make a date for next week.
wǒ-men syà syīng-chī dzài-jyàn ba!
我們下星期再見吧!

53. I have enjoyed myself very much.
wǒ jywé-de hěn kwài-lè! 我覺得很快樂!

54. Give my regards to your [boyfriend] [girlfriend].
chǐng syàng nín [nán péng-you] [nyǔ péng-you] wèn-hou.
請向您[男朋友][女朋友]問候.

BASIC QUESTIONS

55. What? shém-ma? 什麼?

56. What did you say?
nín shwō shém-ma? 您說什麼?

57. What is that? nèi shr̀ shém-ma? 那是什麼?

58. What should I do?
wǒ yīng dzwò shém-ma? 我應做什麼?

59. What is the matter (LIT.: **What is it**)?
shém-ma shr̀? 什麼事?

60. What do you want?
nǐ yàu shém-ma? 你要什麼?

61. What is this? jèi shr̀ shém-ma? 這是什麼?

62. When? shém-ma shŕ-hòu? 什麼時候?

63. Where? dzài năr? 在那兒？

64. Where is it?
nèi-ge dūng-syi dzài năr? 那個東西在那兒？

65. Why? wèi shém-ma? 為什麼？

66. How? dzěm-ma-yàng? 怎麼樣？

67. How long (**time**)**?** dwō jyǒu? 多久？

68. How far? dwō ywǎn? 多遠？

69. How much? dwō-shau? 多少？

70. How many? jǐ-ge? 幾個？

71. How do you do it?
nǐ dzěm-ma-yàng dzwò? 你怎麼樣做？

72. How does it work (LIT.: **Can you tell me how to use this thing**)**?**
chǐng nǐ gàu-sùng wǒ dzěm-ma-yàng yùng jèi-ge dūng-syi? 請你告訴我怎麼樣用這個東西？

73. Who? shéi? 誰？

74. Who are you? nín shì shéi? 您是誰？

75. Who is [that boy]?
[nèi-ge nán-hái-dz] shì shéi? [那個男孩子]是誰？

76. —that girl. —nèi-ge nyǔ-hái-dz. —那個女孩子

77. —this man. —jèi-ge nán-rén. —這個男人.

78. —that woman.
—nèi-ge nyǔ-rén. —那個女人.

79. Am I [on time][early][late]?
wǒ shì-fǒu [jwǔn-shí][tài dzǎu][chí yì-dyǎr]? 我是否[準時][太早][遲一點兒]？

TALKING ABOUT YOURSELF

80. What is your name?
nín gwèi-syìng? 您貴姓？

81. I am [Mr. Smith].
wǒ shr̀ [smith syān-sheng]. 我是［ smith 先生］.

82. My name is [Lisa Foster].
wǒ míng [lisa foster]. 我名［ lisa foster ］.

83. I am [21] years old.
wǒ jīn-nyán [èr-shŕ-yī] swèi. 我今年［二十一］歲.

84. My address is [448 Chang-an Road].
wǒ de dì-jř shr̀ [sz̀-sz̀-bā cháng-an lù].
我的地址是［四四八長安路］.

85. I am [an American citizen].
wǒ shr̀ [měi-gwo gūng-mín]. 我是［美國公民］.

86. —a student. —yí-ge sywé-sheng. 一一個學生.

87. —a teacher. —yí-ge jyàu-ywán. 一一個教員.

88. —a businessman.
yí-ge shāng-rén. 一一個商人.

89. What do you do for a living?
nín dzwò shém-ma shr̀? 您做什麼事？

90. I am a friend of [Mr. Roland].
wǒ shr̀ [roland syān-sheng] de péng-you.
我是［ roland 先生］的朋友.

91. He works for [my firm].
tā dzài [wǒ de gūng-sz̄] dzwò shr̀.
他在［我的公司］做事.

92. I am here [on a vacation].
wǒ dàu jèr lái [syōu-jyà]. 我到這兒來［休假］.

93. —on a business trip.
—dzwò mǎi-mài. 一作買賣.

94. I have been here [one week].
wǒ lái le [yí-ge syīng-chī] le. 我來了[一個星期]了.

95. We plan to stay here until [Friday].
wǒ-men dǎ-swàn dzài jèr jù-dàu [syīng-chī-wǔ].
我們打算在這兒住到[星期五].

96. I am traveling to [Peking].
wǒ yàu dàu [běi-jīng] chyù lyǔ-syíng.
我要到[北京]去旅行.

97. I am in a hurry.
wǒ gǎn-je yàu dzǒu. 我趕着要走.

98. I am [cold] [warm] [hungry] [thirsty].
wǒ jywé-de [lěng] [rè] [è] [kóu kě].
我覺得[冷][熱][餓][口渴].

99. I am [busy] [tired] [happy] [disappointed].
wǒ hěn [máng] [lèi] [gāu-syìng] [shř-wàng].
我很[忙][累][高興][失望].

100. I cannot do it.
nèi-ge wǒ dzwò bu-lyǎu. 那個我做不了.

101. We are [happy] [unhappy] [angry].
wǒ-men hěn [yú-kwài] [bù yú-kwài] [shēng-chì].
我們很[愉快][不愉快][生氣].

MAKING YOURSELF
UNDERSTOOD

102. Do you speak [English]?
nǐ shwō [yīng-wén] ma? 你說[英文]嗎?

103. Where is English spoken?

dzài shém-ma dì-fāng jyǎng yīng-wén?

在 什麼 地方 講 英文?

104. Does anyone here speak [French]?

dzài jèr yǒu-méi-yǒu rén shwō [fà-gwo hwà]?

在 這兒 有沒有 人 說 [法國話]?

105. I read only [Italian].

wǒ jř hwèi nyàn (OR: kàn) [yì-wén].

我 只 會 念 (看) [意文].

106. I speak a little [German].

wǒ hwèi jyǎng yì-dyǎr [dé-gwo hwà].

我 會 講 一點兒 [德國話].

107. Speak more slowly.   chǐng màn yì-dyǎr shwō.   請 慢 一點兒 說.

108. I [do not] understand.

wǒ [bù] dǔng.   我 [不] 懂.

109. Do you understand me?

nǐ dǔng bu-dǔng wǒ shwō shém-ma?

你 懂 不 懂 我 說 什麼?

110. I [do not] know.

wǒ [bù] jř-dàu (OR: wǒ [bù] dǔng).

我 [不] 知道 (我 [不] 懂).

111. I think so. (LIT.: **Probably**).

yé-syǔ.   也 許.

112. Repeat it.   chǐng dzài shwō.   請 再 說.

113. Write it down.   chǐng syě syà lái.   請 寫 下 來.

114. Answer "yes" or "no."   chǐng dá "shř" hwò "bú-shř".請 答 "是" 或 "不是"

115. You are right.   nín dwèi-le.您 對 了.

116. You are wrong.   nín tswò-le.您 錯 了.

117. What is the meaning of [this word]?

[jèi-ge dà] shì shém-ma yì-sà? [這個字]是什麼意思?

118. How do you say ["pencil"] in Chinese?

jūng-gwo hwà nín dzèm-ma-yàng shwō ["pencil"]?

中國話您怎麼樣説 ["pencil"]?

119. How do you spell [that word]?

[nèi-ge dà] shì dzèm-ma-yàng pīn de?

[那個字]是怎麼樣拼的?

DIFFICULTIES AND MISUNDERSTANDINGS

120. Where is [the American embassy]?

[měi-gwo dà-shŕ-gwǎn] dzài nǎr?

[美國大使館]在那兒?

121. —the police station.

—jǐng-chá-jyú. 警察局.

122. —the lost-and-found office.

—shŕ-wù-jàu-lǐng-chù. 一失物報領處.

123. I want to speak to [the manager] [your superior].

wǒ yàu gēn [jīng-lǐ] [shàng-jí] jyǎng-hwà.

我要跟[經理][上級]講話.

124. Can you [help me] [tell me]?

nǐ kě bu ké-yi [bāng wǒ] [gàu-sùng wǒ]?

你可不可以[幫我][告訴我]?

125. I am looking for my [friend].

wǒ dzài jǎu wǒ de [péng-you]. 我在找我的[朋友].

126. I am lost. wǒ mí-lù le. 我迷路了.

127. I cannot find [the address].

wǒ jǎu bú-dàu [nèi-ge dì-jǐ]. 我找不到[那個地址].

128. She has lost [her handbag].

tā shř le [tā de pí-bāu]. 她失了她的皮包].

129. He has lost [his visa].

tā shř le [tā de chyān-jèng]. 他失了[他的簽証].

130. We forgot [our keys].

wǒ-men wàng le [wǒ-men de yàu-shr].
我們忘了[我們的鑰匙].

131. We missed [the train].

wǒ-men méi gǎn-shàng [nèi-bān hwǒ-chē].
我們沒趕上[那班火車].

132. It is not my fault.

jèi bú-shř wǒ de tswò. 這不是我的錯.

133. I do not remember [the name].

wǒ bù jì-de [nèi-ge míng-dz]. 我不記得[那個名字].

134. What is wrong?

yǒu shém-ma bú-dwèi? 有什麼不對?

135. Let us alone!

byé dá-rau (OR: chǎu) wǒ-men! 別打擾(吵)我們!

136. Go away! dzǒu-kāi ba! 走開吧!

137. Help! jyòu-mìng a! 救命呀!

138. Police! jǐng-chá! 警察!

139. Thief! syǎu-tōu! 小偷!

140. Fire! hwǒ-shāu! 火燒!

141. This is an emergency.

jèi shř yí-ge jǐn-jí shr-jyàn. 這是一個緊急事件.

CUSTOMS

142. Where is [the customs office]?
[hǎi-gwān] dzài nǎr? [海關] 在那兒？

143. Here is [our baggage].
[wǒ-men de syíng-li] dzài jèr. [我們的行李] 在這兒。

144. —my passport.
—wǒ de hù-jàu. ─ 我的護照。

145. —my identification card.
—wǒ de shēn-fèn-jèng. ─ 我的身分證。

146. —my health certificate.
—wǒ de jyàn-kāng jèng-shū. ─ 我的健康証書。

147. —my visitor's visa.
—wǒ de yóu-kè chyān-jèng. ─ 我的遊客簽証。

148. I am in transit.
wǒ jǐ shì gwò jìng. 我只是過境。

149. The bags [over there] are mine.
[nèi-byār de] syíng-li shì wǒ de. [那邊兒的] 行李是我的。

150. Must I open everything?
wǒ bì-syū dǎ-kai měi-yí-jyàn ma?
我必需打開每一件嗎？

151. I cannot open [the trunk].
wǒ dǎ bu-kāi [jèi-ge syāng-dz]. 我打不開 [這個箱子]。

152. There is nothing here [but clothing].
lǐ-tou méi-yǒu shém-ma dūng-syi [jyòu yǒu yī-shang].
裏頭沒有什麼東西 [就有衣裳]。

153. I have nothing to declare.
wǒ méi-yǒu shém-ma ké-yi bàu-gwān de.
我沒有什麼可以報官的。

154. Everything is for my personal use.

chywán-bù dōu shr̀ wǒ sz̄-rén yùng de dūng-syi.

全部都是我私人用的東西.

155. I bought [this necklace] in the United States.

[jèi-tyáu syàn-lyàn] wǒ dzài měi-gwo mǎi de.

[這條項鍊] 我在美國買的.

156. These are [gifts].

jèi-syē dōu shr̀ [lǐ-wù]. 這些都是[礼物].

157. This is all I have.

wǒ jǐ yǒu jèi-syē. 我只有這些.

158. Must duty be paid on [these things]?

[jèi-syē dūng-syi] yàu fù gwān-shwèi ma?

[這些東西] 要付關稅嗎?

159. Have you finished [checking]?

[chá] wán le ma? [查] 完了嗎?

BAGGAGE

160. Where can we check our luggage through to [Shanghai]?

dzài shém-ma dì-fāng wǒ-men ké-yi bǎ syíng-li twō yùn dàu [shàng-hǎi]?

在什麼地方我們可以把行李託運到[上海]?

161. These things to the [left] [right] are mine.

dzài [dzwǒ-byār] [yòu-byār] nèi-syē dūng-syi shr̀ wǒ de.

在[左邊兒][右邊兒]那些東西是我的.

162. I cannot find all my baggage.

wǒ jǎu bú dàu chywán-bù de syíng-li.

我找不到全部的行李.

163. [One of my packages] is missing.

[wǒ de yí-jyàn syíng-li] bú jyàn le.

[我的一件行李] 不見了.

164. I want to leave [this suitcase] here [for a few days].

wǒ yàu bǎ [jèi-ge syíng-li] lyóu dzài jèr [jǐ-tyān].

我要把[這個行李]留在這兒[幾天].

165. Give me a receipt for the baggage.

chǐng nín gěi wǒ syíng-li de shōu-tyáur.

請您給我行李的收條.

166. I own [a black trunk].

wǒ yǒu [yí-ge hēi de syāng-dz]. 我有[一個黑的箱子].

167. —four pieces of luggage altogether.

—yí-gùng sž-jyàn syíng-li. 一一共四件行李.

168. Carry these to the baggage room.

chǐng bǎ jèi-syē ná-dàu syíng-li-fáng chyù.

請把這些拿到行李房去.

169. Don't forget that.

bú yàu wàng-ji nèi-ge! 不要忘記那個!

170. I shall carry this myself.

jèi-ge wǒ dž-jǐ ná. 這個我自己拿.

171. Follow me. chǐng gēn-je wǒ lái. 請跟着我來.

172. Get me [a taxi].

chǐng tì wǒ jyàu [yí-bù jì-chéng-chē (OR: te-shř)*].

請替我叫[一部計程車(特士)].

173. —a porter. —yí-ge tyāu-fū. 一一個挑夫.

174. This is very fragile.

jèi-ge hěn tswèi de. 這個很脆的.

175. Handle this carefully.

chǐng syǎu-syīn de tí. 請小心的提.

* In Taiwan, jì-chéng-chē is used; in Hong Kong, te-shř.

176. How much do I owe you?

wǒ yí-gùng chyàn nín dwō-shau chyán?

我一共欠您多少錢？

177. What is the customary tip?

pǔ-tūng shǎng-chyán dwō-shau?   普通賞錢多少？

TRAVEL DIRECTIONS

178. I want to go [to the airline office].

wǒ yàu [dàu háng-kūng gūng-sz̄] chyù.

我要[到航空公司]去．

179. —to the travel bureau.

—dàu lyǔ-syíng shè. 一到旅行社．

180. —to the [Chinese] government tourist office.*

—dàu [jūng-gwo] jèng-fǔ lyǔ-syíng shè.

一到[中國]政府旅行社．

181. How long does it take to walk [to Jung-san Park]?

dzǒu [dàu jūng-sān gūng-ywán] yùng dwō-shau shŕ-hòu?

走[到中山公園]用多少時候？

182. Is this the shortest way [to Fu shan]?

jèi shr̀ bu-shr̀ [dàu fú shān] dzwèi jìn de lù?

這是不是[到佛山]最近的路？

183. Show me the way [to the center of town].

chǐng gàu-sùng wǒ [dàu shr̀-jūng-syīn] dzěm-ma-yàng chyù.

請告訴我[到市中心]怎麼樣去．

184. —to the shopping district.

—dàu shāng-yè chyū. 一到商業區．

* The official travel agency of the People's Republic is simply known as *lyǔ-syíng-shè* (China International Travel Service).

185. Do I turn to the [north] [south] [east] [west]?
shr̀ bu-shr̀ syàng [běi] [nán] [dūng] [syī] jwǎn?
是 不 是 向 [北] [南] [東] [西] 轉 ?

186. What street is this?
jèi-tyáu jyē jyàu shém-ma? 這 條 街 叫 什麼?

187. How far is it? yǒu dwō ywǎn? 有 多 遠 ?

188. Is it near or far?
shr̀ jìn hái-shr̀ ywǎn? 是 近 還 是 遠 ?

189. Can we walk there?
wǒ-men kě bu ké-yi dzǒu lù chyù?
我 們 可 不 可 以 走 路 去 ?

190. Am I going in the right direction?
wǒ dzǒu de fāng-syàng dwèi bu-dwèi?
我 走 的 方 向 對 不 對 ?

191. Please point.
chǐng jǐ gěi wǒ kàn. 請 指 給 我 看.

192. Should I go [this way] [that way]?
wǒ shr̀ bu-shr̀ yàu dzǒu [jèi-byār] [nèi-byār]?
我 是 不 是 要 走 [這邊兒] [那邊兒] ?

193. Turn [left] [right] at the next corner.
dàu dì-èr-ge jyē-kǒu shŕ syàng [dzwǒ] [yòu] jwǎn.
到 第二個 街口 是 向 [左] [右] 轉.

194. Is it [on this side of the street]?
shr̀ bu-shr̀ [dzài jyē-dàu de jèi-byār]?
是 不 是 [在 街道 的 這邊兒] ?

195. —on the other side of the street.
—dzài jyē-dàu de nèi-byār. —在 街道 的 那邊兒.

196. —across the bridge.
—dzài chyáu dwèi-mér. —在 橋 對面 ?

197. —along the boulevard.
—yán dà-mǎ-lù. —沿 大馬路.

198. —between these avenues.
—dzài mǎ-lù jī jyān. 在馬路之間.

199. —beyond the traffic light.
—dzài jyāu-tūng dēng nèi-byār. 在交通燈那边兒.

200. —next to the apartment house.
—dzài gūng-yù de páng-byār. 在公寓的旁边兒.

201. —in the middle of the block.
—dzài yí-lyè fáng-dz de jūng-jyān.
在一列房子的中間.

202. —straight ahead.
—yì-jí syàng chyán dzǒu. 一直向前走.

203. —inside the station.
—dzài chē-jàn de lǐ-tóu. 在車站的裏頭.

204. —near the square.
—dzài gwáng-chǎng de fù-jìn. 在廣場的附近.

205. —outside the lobby.
—dzài dzǒu-láng de wài-myàn. 在走廊的外面.

206. —at the entrance.
—dzài dà-mén-kǒu. 在大門口.

207. —opposite the park.
—dzài gūng-ywán de dwèi-myàn.
在公園的對面.

208. —beside the school.
—dzài sywé-syàu de páng-byār. 在學校的旁边兒.

209. —in front of the monument.
—dzài jì-nyàn-bēi de chyán-myàn.
在紀念碑的前面.

210. —in the rear of the store.
—dzài pù-dz de bèi-hòu. 在鋪子的背後.

211. —behind the building.
—dzài dà-lóu de hòu-myàn. 在大樓的後面.

212. —up the hill.
—dzài shān-shàng. 在山上.

213. —down the stairs.
—dzài lóu-tī syà-myàn. 在樓梯下面.

214. —at the top of the elevator.
—dzài dyàn-tī shàng-tóu. 在電梯上頭.

215. —around the traffic circle.
—ràu-je ywán hwán. 繞着圓環.

216. The factory. gūng-chǎng. 工廠.

217. The office building.
bàn-gūng dà-lóu. 辦公大樓.

218. The residential section.
jù-jè chyū. 住宅區.

219. The city. chéng-shr̀. 城市.

220. The country. syāng-syà. 鄉下.

221. The village. tswūn-dz. 村子.

BOAT

222. When must I go on board?
wǒ shém-ma shŕ-hòu shàng chwán?
我什麼時候上船?

223. Bon voyage! yí-lù shwùn-fēng! 一路順風!

224. I want to rent a deck chair.

wǒ yàu dzū yí-ge rwán yí. 我要租一個軟椅.

225. Can we go ashore at [Kowloon]?

wǒ-men ké-yi dzài [jyǒu-lúng] shàng-àn ma?

我們可以在[九龍]上岸嗎?

226. At what time is dinner served?

wǎn-fàn shém-ma shŕ-hòu kāi-shŕ?

晚飯什麼時候開始?

227. When is the [first sitting] [second sitting]?

[dì-yí-jwō] [dì-èr-jwō] shém-ma shŕ-hòu kāi-shŕ?

[第一桌][第二桌]什麼時候開始?

228. I feel seasick. wǒ jywé-de yūn-chwán. 我覺得暈船.

229. Have you a remedy for seasickness?

nín yǒu méi-yǒu yūn-chwán yàu?

您有沒有暈船藥?

230. Lifeboat. jyòu-shēng-chwán. 救生船.

231. Life preserver.

jyòu-shēng-chywān. 救生圈.

232. The ferry. dù-chwán. 渡船.

233. The dock. mǎ-tou. 碼頭.

234. The cabin. kè-tsāng. 客艙.

235. The deck. jyá-bǎn. 甲板.

236. The gymnasium. tǐ-yù-gwǎn. 体育館.

237. The pool. yóu-yǔng-chŕ. 游泳池.

238. The captain. chwán-jǎng. 船長.

239. The purser.

chwán-shàng de shŕ-wù jǎng. 船上的事務長

240. The cabin steward.
chwán-cháng fú wù shēng. 船艙服務生.

241. The dining room steward.
tsān-tīng fú wù shēng. 餐廳服務生.

AIRPLANE

242. I want [to reserve] [to cancel] an airplane seat.
wǒ syǎng yàu [dìng] [chyǔ-syāu] jī-wèi.
我想要［訂］［取消］机位.

243. What time does the next flight [to Nanking] leave?
[wàng nán-jīng de] syà yí-bān fēi-jī shr̀ jí-dyǎn jūng kāi?
［往南京的］下一班飛机是幾點鐘開？

244. When does the plane arrive at [Tainan]?
fēi-jī shém-ma shŕ-hòu dàu [tái-nán]?
飛机什麼時候到［台南］？

245. What kind of plane is used on that flight?
nèi-bān fēi-jī shr̀ yùng dzěm-ma-yàng de fēi-jī?
那班飛机是用怎麼樣的飛机？

246. Will food be served?
yǒu méi-yǒu tsān kě chŕ? 有沒有餐可吃？

247. May I confirm the reservation by telephone?
wǒ shr̀-fǒu ké-yi dǎ-dyàn-hwà lái chywè-shŕ dìng jī-wèi?
我是否可以打電話來確實訂机位？

248. At what time should we check in at the airport?
wǒ-men syū-yàu shém-ma shŕ-hòu dàu fēi-jī-chǎng dēng-jì?
我們需要什麼時候到飛机場登記？

249. How long does it take to get to the airport from my hotel?

tsúng wǒ de lyú-gwǎn dàu fēi-jī-chǎng syū-yàu dwō-shau shŕ-jyān?

從我的旅館到飛机場需要多少時間？

250. Is there bus service between the airport and the city?

tsúng fēi-jī-chǎng dàu chéng nèi yǒu méi-yǒu gūng-gùng chì-chē?

從飛机場到城內有没有公共汽車？

251. Is that flight nonstop?

nèi-ge bān-jī shŕ bu-shŕ jŕ-dá fēi-syíng?

那個班机是不是直達飛行？

252. Where does the plane stop en route?

fēi-jī dzài jūng-tú tíng dzài nǎr? 飛机在中途停在那兒？

253. How long do we stop?

wǒ-men tíng dwō jyǒu? 我們停多久？

254. May I stop over in [Hangchow]?

wǒ kě bu ké-yi dzài [háng-jōu] tíng-lyóu?

我可不可以在[杭州]停留？

255. We want (to travel) [first class] [economy class].

wǒ-men yàu [tóu-děng] [èr-děng] de.

我們要[頭等][二等]的？

256. Is flight [22] on time?

[èr-shŕ-èr] tsz̀ bān-jī shŕ bu-shŕ jwǔn-shŕ?

[二十二]次班机是不是準時？

257. How much baggage am I allowed?

jwǔn wǒ dài dwō-shau syíng-li? 准我帶多少行李？

258. How much per kilo for excess weight?

chāu jùng měi-gūng-jīn dwō-shau chyán?

超重每公斤多少錢？

259. May I carry this on board?

wǒ kě bu ké-yi bǎ jèi-ge dài shàng-jī?

我可不可以把這個帶上机?

260. Give me a seat [on the aisle].

chǐng gěi wǒ yí-ge [kàu-je dzǒu-dàu de] wèi-dz.

請給我一個[靠着走道的]位子.

261. —by a window.

—kàu-je chwāng kǒu. 一靠着窗口.

262. —by the emergency exit.

—kàu-je ān-chywán mén. 一靠着安全門.

263. May we board the plane now?

syàn-dzài wǒ-men kě bu ké-yi shàng-jī?

現在我們可不可以上机?

264. From which gate does my flight leave?

wǒ dzwò de bān-jī shì tsúng něi-ge jìn-chù kǒu chǐ-fēi?

我坐的班机是従那個進出口起飛?

265. Call the stewardess. chǐng jyàu kūng-jūng syáu-jye. 請叫空中小姐.

266. Fasten your seat belt.

kòu-jǐn nǐ de ān-chywán dài. 扣緊你的安全帶

267. May I smoke?

kě bu ké-yi chōu-yān? 可不可以抽煙?

268. Will we arrive [on time] [late]?

wǒ-men néng bu-néng [jwǔn-shŕ] [chŕ yì-dyǎr] dàu?

我們能不能[準時][遲一點兒]到?

269. An announcement. tūng-gàu. 通告.

270. A boarding pass. shàng-jī-jèng. 上机證

271. The limousine.

háu hwǎ jyàu-chē. 豪華轎車.

TRAIN

272. When does the ticket office [open] [close]?
shòu-pyàu-chù shém-ma shŕ-hòu [kāi] [gwān]?
售票處什麼時候[開][關]?

273. When is the next train for [Syi-an]?
wàng [syī-án de] syà yi-bān hwŏ-chē shém-ma shŕ-hòu kāi?
往[西安的]下一班火車什麼時候開?

274. Is there [an earlier train]?
yŏu méi-yŏu [dzăo yì-dyăr de hwŏ-chē]?
有沒有[早一點兒的火車]?

275. —a later train.
—chŕ yì-dyăr de hwŏ-chē. -遲一點兒的火車.

276. —an express train.   —kwài chē. - 快車.

277. —a local train.   —màn chē. - 慢車.

278. From which track (OR: platform) does the train leave?
hwŏ-chē tsúng něi-ge tái lí-kāi? 火車從那個胎離開?

279. Where can I get a timetable?
shém-ma dì-fāng ké-yi ná dàu shŕ-jyān byău?
什麼地方可以拿到時間表?

280. Does this train stop at [Chung-ching]?
jèi-jyà hwŏ-chē dzài [chúng-ching] tíng bu tíng?
這架火車在[重广]停不停?

281. Is there time to get off?
yŏu méi-yŏu shŕ-jyān syà-chē? 有沒有時間下車?

282. When do we arrive?
wŏ-men shém-ma shŕ-hòu dàu? 我們什麼時候到?

283. Is this seat taken (LIT.: Is someone sitting in this seat)?

jèi-ge wèi-dz yǒu méi-yǒu rén dzwò?

這個位子有沒有人坐？

284. Am I disturbing you?

wǒ yǒu méi-yǒu dá-jyǎu nín? 我有沒有打攪您？

285. Open the window.

chǐng kāi chwāng-hù. 請開窗户

286. Close the door.

chǐng gwān mén. 請關門．

287. Where are we now?

wǒ-men syàn-dzài dzài nǎr? 我們現在在那兒？

288. Is the train on time?

hwǒ-chē shɿ bu-shɿ jwǔn-shɿ? 火車是不是準時？

289. How late are we?

wǒ-men chɿ le dwō jyǒu? 我們遲了多久？

290. The conductor. lyè-chē-jǎng. 列車長

291. The gate. jyǎn-pyàu kǒu. 剪票口

292. The information office (OR: booth).

wèn-syùn-chù. 問詢處

293. A [one-way] [round-trip] ticket.

[dān-chéng] [lái-hwéi] pyàu. [單程] [來回] 票

294. The porter. húng-máu-dz. 紅帽子

295. The railroad station.

hwǒ-chē-jàn. 火車站．

296. The waiting room.

hòu-chē-shɿ. 候車室

297. The sleeping car. wò-chē. 臥車

298. A bedroom compartment (OR: **roomette**).

wò-shr̀ yùng de fáng-jyān. 臥室用的房間.

299. The smoking car.

chōu-yān-chē. 抽煙車.

300. The dining car.   fàn-chē. 飯車.

BUS, SUBWAY AND STREETCAR

301. Where does [the streetcar] stop?

[dyàn-chē] tíng dzài năr? [電車] 停在那兒?

302. How often does [the subway] run?

[dì syà hwó-chē] yì-tyān kāi dwō-shau-tsz̀? [地下火車] 一天開多少次?

303. Which bus goes to [Gau-syung]?

shém-ma gūng-gùng chì-chē dàu [gāu-syúng] chyù? 什麼公共汽車到 [高雄] 去?

304. How much is the fare?

chē-pyàu dwō-shau chyán? 車票多少錢?

305. Do you go near [West Lake]?

nín dàu bu dàu [syī-hú] fù-jìn? 您到不到 [西湖] 附近?

306. I want to get off [at the next stop] [right here].

wǒ yàu [dzài syà yí-jàn] [dzài jèr] syà-chē. 我要 [在下一站] [在這兒] 下車.

307. Please tell me where to get off.

chǐng gàu-sùng wǒ dzài năr syà-chē. 請告訴我在那兒下車.

308. Will I have to change?

wǒ yàu bu yàu hwàn chē? 我要不要換車?

309. Where do we transfer?
wǒ-men dzài nǎr hwàn chē? 我們在那兒換車?

310. The driver. sž-jī. 司机

311. The transfer. hwàn chē pyàu. 換車票

312. The token. dài yùng hwò bèi. 代用貨幣

313. The conductor. chē-shǎng. 車賞

314. The bus stop.
gūng-gùng chì-chē-jàn. 公共汽車站

TAXI

315. Call a taxi for me.
chǐng tì wǒ jyàu yí-lyàng chù-dzū de chì-chē.
請替我叫一輛出租的汽車

316. Are you free, driver?*
sž-jī, nín yǒu kùng ma? 司机, 您有空嗎?

317. What do you charge [per hour]?
[měi-ge jūng-tóu] dwō-shaу chyán?
[每個鐘頭] 多少錢?

318. —per kilometer.
—měi-gūng-lǐ. 每公里

319. Take me to this address. 請送我到這個地址
chǐng sùng wǒ dàu jèi-ge dì-jř.

* See note on p. 3.

320. How much will the ride cost?

chéng-yí-tsż yàu dwō-shau chyán?

乘 一 次 要 多 少 錢 ？

321. How long will it take to get there?

dàu nàr syū-yàu dwō-shau shŕ-jyān?

到 那兒 需要 多少 時間 ？

322. Drive us around [for one hour].

swéi-byàn kāi [yí-ge jūng-tóu].　隨便 開 [一個鐘頭].

323. Drive more carefully.

gèng syău-syīn de kāi　更 小 心 的 開 .

324. Drive more slowly.

gèng màn-màr de kāi　更 慢 慢 的 開 .

325. I am not in a great hurry.

wǒ bù gǎn shŕ-jyān　我 不 趕 時間 .

326. Stop here.　chǐng tíng dzài jèr.　請 停 在 這兒 .

327. Wait for me here.

chǐng dzài jèr děng wǒ.　請 在 這兒 等 我 .

328. I will return in [five minutes].

[wǔ-fēn jūng] yǐ-hòu wǒ jyòu hwéi-lái.

[五分鐘] 以後 我 就 回 來 .

329. Keep the change.

líng chyán gěi nín.　零 錢 給 您 .

330. The taxi stand.

jì-chéng-chē-jàn.　計 程 車 站 .

331. The taxi meter.　jì-swàn-byǎu.　計 算 錶 .

332. A licensed taxi.

yǒu pái-jàu jì-chéng-chē.　有 牌 照 計 程 車 .

RENTING AUTOS AND OTHER VEHICLES

333. What kind of [cars] do you have?

nǐ de [chē] shǐ něi-yi-jǔng? 你的[車]是那一種？

334. I have an international driver's license.

wǒ yǒu gwó-jì jyà-shǐ jí-jau. 我有國際駕駛執照.

335. What is the rate [per day]?

[měi-tyān de] jyà-gé dwō-shau chyán?

[每天的]價格多少錢？

336. How much additional [per kilometer]?

[yí-gūng-lǐ] jyā dwō-shau chyán?

[一公里]加多少錢？

337. Are gas and oil also included?

chì-yóu gēn hwá-yóu shǐ-fǒu dōu bāu-gwà dzài nèi?

汽油跟滑油是否都包括在內？

338. Does the insurance policy cover [personal liability]?

báu-syǎn-gūng-sž shǐ-fǒu dān-bǎu [sž-rén dzài-wù]?

保險公司是否担保[私人債務]？

339. —property damage.

—tsái-chǎn swǔn-shī. 一財産損失.

340. —collision.   —jwàng chē. 一撞車

341. Are the papers in order?

shǒu-syù dōu yù-bei hǎu le ma? 手續多務備好了嗎?

342. I am not familiar with this car.

wǒ dwèi jèi-bù chē bú-dà shú-shr.

我對這部車不大熟悉.

343. Explain [this dial].

chǐng jyě-shr [jèi-ge byǎu-pán]. 請解釋[這個標盤]

344. —this mechanism,

—jèi-ge jī-jyè jyé-gòu. -這個机械結構.

345. Show me how [the heater] operates.

chǐng nín shwō-míng [jèi-ge rwán-chì-jī] shr̀ dzěm-ma-yàng kāi-dùng de.

請您説明[這個暖氣机]是怎麼樣的開動的?

346. Will someone pick it up at the hotel?

shr̀-fǒu yǒu-rén kě dàu lyú-gwǎn chyù ná?

是否有人可到旅館去拿?

347. Is the office open all night?

bàn-shr̀-chù shr̀-fǒu jěng yè kāi-je?

辦事處是否整夜開着?

348. The bicycle. dz̀-syíng-chē. 自行車.

349. The motorcycle. mó-twō-chē. 摩托車.

350. The motor scooter.

mó-twō-pǎu-chē. 摩托跑車

351. The horse and wagon.

mǎ gēn mǎ-chē. 馬跟馬車.

AUTO: DIRECTIONS

352. What is the name of [this city]?

[jèi-ge chéng-shr̀] jyàu shém-ma míng-dz?

[這個城市]叫什麼名字?

353. How far [to the next town]?

[dàu syà yí-ge shr̀] hái yǒu dwō ywǎn?

[到下一個市]還有多遠?

354. Where does [this road] lead?

[jèi-tyáu lù] dàu nǎr chyù?

[這條路]到那兒去?

355. Are there road signs?
yǒu méi-yǒu lù-byāu? 有沒有路標？

356. Is the road [paved] [rough]?
shr bu-shr [shwěi-ní] [bù-píng de] lù? 是不是 [水泥] [不平的] 路？

357. Show me the easiest way.
chǐng gàu-sùng wǒ dzwèi jyǎn-dān de lù dzǒu.
請告訴我最簡單的路走．

358. Point it out to me on this road map.
chǐng dzài jèi dì-tú shàng jǐ gěi wǒ kàn.
請在這地圖上指給我看．

359. Can I avoid heavy traffic?
wǒ kě bu ké-yi bì-myǎn jyāu-tūng yūng-jǐ? 我可不可以避免交通擁擠？

360. May I park here [for a while] [overnight]?
wǒ kě [jàn-shŕ] [yǐ-yè] tíng dzài jèr ma? 我可 [暫時] [一夜] 停在這兒嗎？

361. The approach. jìn-lù. 進路．

362. The expressway.
gāu-sù gūng-lù. 高速公路．

363. The fork. chà-dàu. 岔道

364. The intersection. shŕ-dż lù-kǒu. 十字路口

365. The major road. jǔ-yàu-lù. 主要路．

366. The garage. chē-fáng. 車房．

367. The auto repair shop.
chì-chē syōu-lǐ-fáng. 汽車修理房．

368. The parking lot.
tíng-chē-chǎng. 停車場．

369. The stop sign. tíng-chē-byāu. 停車標．

AUTO: HELP ON THE ROAD

370. My car has broken down.
wǒ de chì-chē hwài le. 我的汽車壞了.

371. Call a (car) mechanic.
chǐng jyàu yí-ge syōu-chē-jyàng. 請叫一個修車匠.

372. Help me push [the car] to the side.
chǐng bāng wǒ bǎ [jèi-bu chì-chē] twēi dàu páng-byān.
請幫我把[這部汽車]推到旁邊兒.

373. Push me. twēi wǒ. 推我.

374. May I borrow [a jack]?
wǒ syǎng jyè [yí-ge chǐ-jùng-jī]. 我想借[一個起重机].

375. Change the tire.
chǐng jyāng chē-tāi hwàn yí-syà. 請將車胎換一下.

376. My car is stuck [in the mud].
wǒ de chì-chē [gěi ní-jyāng] swǒ bàn-jù.
我的汽車[給泥漿]所絆住.

377. —in the ditch.
—chūng lwò gōu nèi. 一衝落溝內.

378. Drive me to the nearest [gas station].
chǐng dài wǒ dàu dzwèi jìn de [chì-yóu-jàn].
請帶我到最近的[汽油站].

AUTO: GAS STATION AND
REPAIR SHOP

379. Give me [twenty] liters of [regular] [premium] gasoline.
chǐng gěi wǒ [èr-shí] gūng-shēng de [píng-cháng] [gāu-jí] chì-yóu.
請給我[二十]公升的[平常][高級]汽油.

380. Fill it up.

chǐng bǎ tā jwāng mǎn. 請把它裝滿.

381. Change the oil.

chǐng hwàn-hwàn hwá-yóu. 請換換滑油.

382. Lubricate the car.

chǐng dzài chē shàng jwāng hwá-yóu.

請在車上裝滑油.

383. [Light] [Medium] [Heavy-weight] oil.

[chǐng de] [jūng-děng de] [jùng-lyàng jí de] hwá-yóu.

[輕的] [中等的] [重量級的] 滑油.

384. Put water in the radiator.

chǐng bǎ shwěi fàng dzài shwěi-syāng.

請把水放在水箱.

385. Recharge the battery.

chǐng bǎ dyàn-chí dzài chūng-dyàn.

請把電池再充電.

386. Clean the windshield.

chǐng bǎ dǎng-fēng bwō-li tsā gān-jìng.

請把擋風玻璃擦乾淨.

387. Adjust [the brakes].

chǐng bǎ [shā-chē] tyáu hǎu. 請把[剎車]調好.

388. Check the tire pressure.

chǐng chá yí-syà chē-lwún kàn gòu bu-gòu chì.

請查一下車輪看夠不夠氣

389. Repair the flat tire.

chǐng bǎ méi-chì de lwún-tāi syōu-lǐ yí-syà.

請把沒氣的輪胎修理一下.

390. Could you wash it [now]?

nín kě bu ké-yi [syàn-dzài] bǎ tā syǐ-yi-syǐ?

您可不可以[現在]把它洗一洗?

391. How long must we wait?
wǒ-men syū-yàu děng dwō jyǒu? 我們需要等多久？

392. The motor overheats.
fā-dùng-jī tài rè le! 發動机太熱了！

393. Is there a leak?
yǒu méi-yǒu lòu-dùng? 有沒有漏洞？

394. It makes a noise. hén chǎu. 很吵。

395. The lights do not work.
chē dēng hwài le. 車燈壞了。

396. The car does not start.
jèi-bù chì-chē bu-néng fā-dùng. 這部汽車不能發動

PARTS OF THE CAR AND AUTO EQUIPMENT

397. Accelerator.
jyā-sù-chì (OR: yóu-mén). 加速器（油門）。

398. Air filter. kūng-chì gwò-lyù-chì. 空氣過濾器

399. Alcohol. jyǒu-jīng. 酒精。

400. Antifreeze. fáng-dùng-jì. 防凍劑。

401. Axle. chē-jóu. 車軸。

402. Battery. dyàn-chŕ. 電池。

403. Bolt. lwó-sz-dīng. 螺絲釘。

404. Brakes. shā-chē. 刹車。

405. Bulb (light). dēng-pàu. 燈泡。

06. Emergency brake. ḿn-jí-shā-chē. 緊急刹車.

07. Foot brake. jyǎu-shā-chē. 脚刹車.

08. Hand brake. shǒu-shā-chē. 手刹車.

09. Bumper. fáng-jwàng-gùng. 防撞拱.

10. Carburetor. tàn-hwà-chì. 碳化器.

11. Chassis. chē-pán. 車盤.

12. Choke (automatic). bì-sè-bù. 閉塞部.

13. Clutch. lí-hé-chì. 離合器.

14. Cylinder. chì-gāng. 汽缸.

15. Differential. chà-dùng-chì. 差動器.

16. Directional signal. ḿn-hàu-jǐ-syàng-chì. 信号指向器.

17. Door. mén. 門.

18. Electrical system. ḿyàn-chì-syì-tǔng. 電氣系統.

19. Engine. jī-chì. 机器.

20. Exhaust pipe. pái-chì-gwǎn. 排氣管.

21. Exterior. wài-bù-de. 外部的.

22. Fan. fēng-shàn. 風扇.

23. Fan belt. fēng-shàn-dài. 風扇帶.

24. Fender. dǎng-ní-bān. 擋泥板.

25. Flashlight. shǒu-dyàn-tǔng. 手電筒.

26. Fuel pump. rán-chì-tǔng. 燃氣筒.

27. Fuse. báu-syǎn-syī. 保險絲.

428. Gear shift. byàn-sù-chì. 變速器

429. First gear. dì-yī-sù. 第一速

430. Second gear. dì-èr-sù. 第二速

431. Third gear. dì-sān-sù. 第三速

432. Fourth gear. dì-sż-sù. 第四速

433. Reverse gear. dàu-chē. 倒車

434. Neutral gear. kūng-dwàn. 空段

435. Generator. fā-dyàn-jī. 發電机

436. Grease. hwáng-yóu. 黃油

437. Hammer. chwéi-dz. 鎚子

438. Hood. jī-chì gài. 机器蓋

439. Horn. (chē) lǎ-ba. (車)喇叭

440. Horsepower. mǎ-lì. 馬力

441. Ignition key. chǐ-dùng yàu-shr. 起動鑰匙

442. Inner tube. nèi-tāi. 內胎

443. Instrument panel. yí-chì-bǎn. 儀器板

444. License plate. chē-pái. 車牌

445. Light. dēng. 燈

446. Headlight. chyán-dēng. 前燈

447. Parking light. tíng-chē-dēng. 停車燈

448. Brake light. shā-chē-dēng. 剎車燈

449. Taillight. wěi-dēng. 尾燈

450. Lubrication system.
hwá-rwùn jǔ-jī. 滑潤組織

451. Rear-view mirror.
hòu-wàng-jìng. 後望鏡.

452. Side-view mirror.
páng-wàng-jìng. 旁望鏡.

453. Motor. fā-dùng-jī. 發動机.

454. Muffler. myè-yīn-chì. 滅音器.

455. Nail. dīng. 釘.

456. Nut. lwó-màu. 螺帽.

457. Oil. yóu. 油.

458. Pedal. tà-bǎn. 踏板.

459. Pliers. chyán-dz. 鉗子.

460. Radiator. lěng-chywè-chì. 冷卻器.

461. Radio. wú-syàn-dyàn. 無綫電.

462. Rags. mwó-bù. 抹布.

463. Rope. shéng-dz. 繩子.

464. Screw. lwó-sz-dīng. 螺絲釘.

465. Screwdriver. lwó-sz-chí-dz. 螺絲起子.

466. Shock absorber. jyǎn-jèn-chì. 減震器.

467. Skid chains. fáng-hwá-tyě-lyàn. 防滑鐵鍊.

468. Snow tires. syà-sywě-lwún-tāi. 下雪輪胎.

469. Spark plugs. hwǒ sè. 火塞.

470. Speedometer. sù-dù-jì. 速度計.

471. Spring. tán-hwáng. 彈簧.

472. Starter. mǎ-dá. 馬達.

473. Steering wheel.
fāng-syàng-pán. 方向盤.

474. Tank. chì-yóu-syāng. 汽油箱.

475. Spare tire. yù-bèi-lwún-tāi. 預備輪胎.

476. Tubeless tire. yìng-chē-tāi. 硬車胎.

477. Tire pump. dǎ-chì-tǔng. 打氣筒.

478. Tools. gūng-jyù. 工具.

479. Automatic transmission.
dž-dùng-byàn-sù. 自動變速.

480. Standard transmission.
shǒu-byàn-sù. 手變速.

481. Trunk. syíng-li-syāng. 行李箱.

482. Valve. hwó-mén. 活門.

483. Water-cooling system.
shwéi-lěng-fǎ. 水冷法.

484. Front wheel. chyán-lwún. 前輪.

485. Rear wheel. hòu-lwún. 後輪.

486. Windshield wiper.
dǎng-fēng-bwō-li-shwā. 擋風玻璃刷.

487. Wrench. bǎn-tóu. 扳頭.

MAIL

488. Where is [the post office]?
[yóu-jèng-jyú] dzài nǎr?
[郵政局] 在那兒?

489. —a mailbox. —syìn-syāng. 一信箱.

490. To which window should I go?

wǒ syū-yàu dàu něi-ge chwāng-kǒu?

我需要到那個窗口？

491. I want to send this letter [by surface mail].

wǒ yàu [yùng píng-syìn-yóu] jì jèi-fēng syìn.

我要[用平信郵]寄這封信.

492. —by airmail.

—yùng háng-kūng-jì. 一用航空寄.

493. —by special delivery.

—yùng tè-byé jwān-sùng. 一用特別專送.

494. —by registered mail, reply requested.

—yùng shwāng-gwà-hàu-jì. 一用双掛号寄.

495. —by parcel post.

—yùng yóu-bāu-jì. 一用郵包寄.

496. How much postage do I need [for this postcard]?

[jèi-jāng míng-syìn-pyàn] syū-yàu dwō-shau yóu-pyàu?

[這張明信片]需要多少郵票？

497. The package contains [printed matter].

jèi bāu-gwǒ lǐ sh̀ [yìn-shwā-pǐn].

這包裹裡是[印刷品].

498. —fragile material.

—yì-swèi de wù-pǐn. 一易碎的物品.

499. I want to insure this for [fifty ywan].*

wǒ yàu bǎ jèi-ge dūng-syi báu-syǎn [wǔ-shŕ-ywán].

我要把這個東西保險[五十圓].

---

* The currency system of the People's Republic is: 100 *fēn* =
10 *jyǎu* (or: *máu*) = 1 *ywán*. 1 *ywán* (¥1) was worth roughly $.60 in
1979. The currency of Taiwan, the New Taiwan Dollar, was
equal to $.03.

500. Give me a receipt.
chǐng gěi wǒ shōu-tyáu. 請給我收條.

501. Will it go out [today]?
[jǐn-tyān] néng bu néng sùng chū-chyù? [今天] 能不能送出去?

502. Give me ten [22-fen] stamps.
chǐng gěi wǒ shŕ-jāng [èr-shŕ-èr-fēn de] yóu-pyàu.
請給我十張 [二十二分的] 郵票.

503. Where can I get [a money order]?
wǒ dzài nǎr néng gòu mǎi-dàu [hwèi-pyàu]?
我在那兒能够買到 [匯票]?

504. Please forward my mail to [Tai-jung University].
chǐng jyāng wǒ de syìn-jyàn jwǎn jì-gěi dàu [tài-jūng dà-sywé].
請將我的信件轉寄給到 [台中大學]

505. [The American Express office] will hold my mail.
[měi-gwo kwài shwèi gūng-sž] tì wǒ dài-shōu syìn-jyàn.
[美國快兌公司] 替我代收信件.

TELEGRAM

506. I would like to send [a telegram].
wǒ syǎng yàu dǎ [yí-ge dyàn-bàu].
我想要打 [一個電報].

507. —a night letter.
—yè-jyān màn-fā cháng-dyàn-bàu.
一夜間慢發長電報.

508. —a cablegram.
—hǎi-wài-dyàn-bàu. 一海外電報.

509. What is the rate per word?

měi-ge dz̀ dwō-shau chyán? 每個字多少錢？

510. What is the minimum charge?

dzwèi dī dài-jyà dwō-shau chyán?

最低代價多少錢？

511. When will an ordinary cablegram reach [Hong Kong]?

pǔ-tūng hǎi-wài-dyàn-bàu shém-ma shŕ-hòu néng dàu-dá [syāng gáng]?

普通海外電報什麼時候能到達[香港]？

TELEPHONE

512. May I use the telephone?

jyè-yùng dyàn-hwà yí-syà! 借用電話一下

513. Will you dial this number for me?*

chǐng tì wǒ bwō jèi-ge dyàn-hwà-hàu-mǎ.

請替我撥這個電話號碼.

514. Call me at this number. 您打這個號碼找我.

nín dǎ jèi-ge hàu-mǎ jǎu wǒ.

515. My telephone number is [884121].

wǒ de dyàn-hwà-hàu-mǎ shr̀ [bā-bā-sz̀-yī-èr-yī].

我的電話號碼是[八八四一二一]

516. How much is a long-distance call to [New York]?

dǎ-dàu [nyǒu-ywe] de cháng-tú dyàn-hwà dwō-shau chyán?

打到[紐約]的長途電話多少錢？

---

* This Chinese sentence can also be used to express the idea: "Operator, please get me this number."

517. What is the charge for the first three minutes?

tóu sān-fēn-jūng dwō-shau chyán?

跟 三 分 鐘 多 少 錢？

518. I want to reverse the charges (LIT.: **I want the other party to pay the charges**).

wǒ yàu dwèi-fāng fù chyán. 我 要 對 方 付 錢.

519. Please bill me at my home phone number.

chǐng jì dzài wǒ jyā dyàn-hwà-hàu-mǎ jàng shàng.

請 記 在 我 家 電 話 号 碼 賬 上.

520. They do not answer.

méi-yǒu rén jyē dyàn-hwà. 没 有 人 接 電 話.

521. The line is busy.

jèi-ge dyàn-hwà-hàu-mǎ yǒu rén dzài yùng.

這 個 電 話 号 碼 有 人 在 用.

522. Hello (**on the telephone**). wèi. 喂.

523. You have given me the wrong number.

nín gěi wǒ de dyàn-hwà-hàu-mǎ bú-dwèi.

您 给 我 的 電 話 号 碼 不 對.

524. This is [Mrs. Norris] speaking.

wǒ shr̀ [norris tài-tai]. 我 是 [norris 太 太].

525. With whom do you want to speak?

nín yàu gēn shéi jyǎng-hwà? 您 要 跟 誰 講 話？

526. Hold the line. chǐng děng yí-syà. 請 等 一 下.

527. Dial again.

chǐng dzài bwō yí-tsz̀. 請 再 撥 一 次.

528. I cannot hear you.

wǒ tīng-bu-jyàn. 我 聽 不 見.

529. The connection is poor.

tūng-hwà chíng-syíng bu dà hǎu.

通 話 情 形 不 大 好.

530. Speak louder.

chǐng shwō dà-shēng yì-dyǎr. 請說大聲一點兒

531. Call her to the phone.

chǐng jyàu tā lái tīng dyàn-hwà. 請叫她來聽電話

532. He is not here.　tā bu dzài jèr. 他不在這兒

533. You are wanted on the telephone.

yǒu nǐ de dyàn-hwà (OR: yǒu rén dǎ dyàn-hwà jǎu nǐ).

有你的電話（有人打電話找你）.

534. May I leave a message?

wǒ kě bu ké-yi lyóu yí-ge dž-tyáu?

我可不可以留一個字條？

535. Call me back.　chǐng dzài dǎ lái. 請再打來

536. I will call back later.

wǒ děng yí-syà dzài dǎ. 我等一下再打.

537. I will wait for your call until [eight] o'clock.

wǒ dzài [bā] dyǎn yǐ-chyán děng nín de dyàn-hwà.

我在[八]點以前等您的電話.

HOTEL

538. I am looking for [a good hotel].

wǒ dzài jǎu [yí-ge hǎu de lyú-gwǎn].

我在找 [一個好的旅館].

539. —the best hotel.　dǐng hǎu de lyú-gwǎn. 一頂好的旅館.

540. —an inexpensive hotel.

—yí-jyā pyán-yì de lyú-gwǎn. 一家便宜的旅館.

541. —a boarding house (OR: pension).

—yì-swǒ gūng-yù. 一一所公寓.

542. I want to be in the center of town.

wǒ yàu dzài shr̀-jūng-syīn. 我要在市中心.

543. I want a quiet location.

wǒ yàu yí-ge ān-jìng de dì-chyū. 我要一個安靜的地區

544. I prefer to be close to [the university].

wǒ syǐ-hwān jù kàu jìn [dà-sywé].
我喜歡住靠近[大學].

545. I have reserved a room for tonight.

wǒ dìng le jīn-tyān wǎn-shàng de rén-fáng.
我訂了今天晚上的人房

546. Where is the registration desk?

děng-jì-chù dzài nǎr? 登記處在那兒?

547. Fill out this registration form.

chǐng tyán shàng jèi-jāng děng-jì-byǎu.
請填上這張登記表

548. Sign here, please.

chǐng chyān-míng. 請簽名.

549. Leave your passport.

chǐng bǎ nín de hù-jàu lyóu-syà. 請把您的護照留下

550. Pick it up later.

děng yì-hwěr lái ná. 等一會兒來拿.

551. Do you have [a single room]?

nín yǒu méi-yǒu [dān-rén-fáng]? 您有沒有[單人房]?

552. —a double room.

—shwāng-rén-fáng. 一雙人房

553. —an air-conditioned room.

—lěng-chì fáng-jyān. 一冷氣房間

554. —a suite. —tàu-fáng. 套房.

555. —an inside room.
—syàng nèi de fáng-jyān. - 向内的房間．

556. —an outside room.
—syàng wài de fáng-jyān. - 向外的房間

557. —a room with a pretty view.
—yǒu hǎu jǐng-sè de fáng-jyān. 有好景色的房間．

558. I want a room with [a double bed].
wǒ yàu yì-jyān fáng-dz dài yǒu [shwāng-rén chwáng de].
我要一間房子帶有 [双人床的]．

559. —twin beds (LIT.: **a single bed**).
—dān-rén chwáng de. - 單人床的．

560. —bath.   —yù-shř de. - 浴室的

561. —shower.   —lìn-yù. - 淋浴．

562. —running water.
—dž-lái shwěi. - 自來水

563. —hot water.   —rè shwěi. - 熱水

564. —balcony.   —lù-tái. - 露台

565. —television.   —dyàn-shr̀. -電視．

566. I shall take a room [for one night].
wǒ yàu yí-ge fáng-jyān jř jù [yí-yè de].
我要一個房間只住 [一夜的]．

567. —for several days.
—jǐ-tyān de. - 幾天的．

568. —for about a week.
—chà-bu-dwō yí-ge lǐ-bài (OR: syīng-chī) de.
- 差不多一個禮拜 (星期) 的．

569. —for two persons.
—lyǎng-ge rén de. - 兩個人的．

570. Can I have a room [with meals]?

wǒ néng yǒu gé [dài fàn] fáng-jyān?

我能有間［帶飯］房間？

571. —without meals.

—bù dài fàn. — 不帶飯.

572. —with breakfast only.

—jř bāu-kwò dzǎu-tsān. — 只包括早餐.

573. What is the rate per [night] [week] [month]?

yí-ge [wǎn-shàng] [syīng-chī] [ywè] dwō-shau chyán?

一個［晚上］［星期］［月］多少錢？

574. Are tax and service included?

shwèi gēn syǎu-fèi yě jyā shàng le ma?

税跟小費也加上了嗎？

575. I would like to see the room.

wǒ syǎng kàn-kàn nèi-ge fáng-jyān.

我想看看那個房間.

576. Have you something [better]?

nín yǒu méi-yǒu [gèng hǎu] de? 您有沒有［更好］的？

577. —cheaper.   —gèng pyán-yì. 更便宜.

578. —larger.   —gèng dà. — 更大.

579. —smaller.   —gèng syǎu. — 更小.

580. —on a [lower] [higher] floor.

—dzài [dǐ yì-tséng] [gāu yì-tséng] lóu.

— 在［底一層］［高一層］樓.

581. —with more light.

—lyàng yì-dyǎr. — 亮一點兒.

582. —with more air.

—kūng-chì lyóu-tūng yì-dyǎr. — 空氣流通一點.

583. —more attractively furnished.

—bǐ-jyàu bù-jr de gèng pyàu-lyàng.

比較佈置的更漂亮．

584. —with a view of the sea.

—ké-yǐ kàn dàu hái-jǐng. 可以看到海景．

585. It's too noisy.   tài chǎu le. 太吵了！

586. This is satisfactory.

wǒ hén mǎn-dzú. 我很滿足．

587. Is there [an elevator]?

yǒu méi-yǒu [dyàn-tī]? 有没有 [電梯]？

588. Upstairs.   lóu-shàng. 樓上．

589. Downstairs.   lóu-syà. 樓下．

590. What is my room number?

wǒ de fáng-jyān jǐ-hàu? 我的房間幾号？

591. Give me my room key.

chǐng gěi wǒ fáng-jyān de yàu-shr.

請給我房間的鑰匙．

592. Bring my luggage upstairs.

chǐng bǎ wǒ de syíng-lǐ dài-dàu lóu-shàng chyù.

請把我的行李帶到樓上去．

593. Tell the chambermaid to get my room ready.

chǐng gàu-sùng nyǚ-shr̀-jě bǎ wǒ de fáng-jyān jéng-lǐ yí-syà.

請告訴女侍者把我的房間整理一下．

594. Wake me [at eight in the morning].

chǐng [dzǎu-shàng bā-dyǎn-jūng] bǎ wǒ jyàu-syǐng.

請 [早上八點鐘] 把我叫醒．

595. Do not disturb me until then.

bú-dàu nèi-ge shŕ-hòu bú-yàu dá-rǎu wǒ.

不到那個時候不要打擾我．

596. I want [breakfast] in my room.

wǒ yàu [dzǎu-tsān] sùng-dàu wǒ de fáng-jyān lái.

我要[早餐]送到我的房間來．

597. Room service, please.

wǒ yǒu yì-dyǎr shÿ (OR: chǐng fù-wù-ywán lái yí-syà).

我有一點兒事（請服務員來一下）．

598. Please bring me [some ice cubes].

chǐng gěi wǒ [yì-syē bīng-kwài]. 請給我[一些冰塊]．

599. Have you [a letter] [message] [parcel] for me?

nín yǒu méi-yǒu [syìn-jyàn] [dž-tyáu] [yóu-bāu] gěi wǒ?

您有沒有[信件][字條][郵包]給我．

600. Send [a chambermaid],

chǐng jyàu [nyǔ-shÿ-jě] lái. 請叫[女侍者]來．

601. —a valet. —shÿ-pú. 一侍僕

602. —a bellhop. —húng-máu-dz. 一紅帽子

603. —a waiter. —shÿ-jě. 一侍者

604. —a messenger. —sùng-syìn jě. 一送信者

605. I am expecting a [friend] [telephone call].

wǒ dzài děng-hòu yí-ge [péng-you] [dyàn-hwà].

我在等候一個[朋友][電話]

606. Has anyone called?

yǒu méi-yǒu rén dǎ dyàn-hwà lái jǎu wǒ?

有沒有人打電話來找我？

607. Send him up.

chǐng gàu-sùng tā shàng lái. 請告訴他上來．

608. I shall not be back for lunch.

wǒ bù hwéi lái chÿ wǔ-fàn. 我不回來吃午飯．

609. May I leave [these valuables] in the hotel safe?

wǒ shì-fǒu ké-yi jyāng [jèi-syē gwèi-jùng wù] lyóu dzài lyú-gwǎn de báu-syǎn-syāng? 我是否可以將[這些貴重物]留在旅館的保險箱?

610. I would like to get my possessions from the safe.

wǒ syǎng yàu ná wǒ lyóu dzài báu-syǎn-syāng de dūng-syi. 我想要拿我留在保險箱的東西.

611. When must I check out?

wǒ syū-yàu shém-ma shí-hòu fù-jàng bān-chū-chyù? 我需要什麼時候付賬搬出去?

612. I am leaving [at 10 o'clock].

wǒ [shí-dyǎn-jūng] dzǒu. 我[十點鐘]走.

613. Make out my bill [as soon as possible].

chǐng [gǎn-kwài] bǎ wǒ de jàng-dān syě-chū-lái. 請[趕快]把我的帳單寫出來

614. The cashier. chū-nà-ywán. 出納員.

615. The doorman. kàn-mén de rén. 看門的人.

616. The lobby. dzǒu-láng. 走廊.

CHAMBERMAID

617. The door doesn't lock.

jèi-ge mén bú néng swǒ. 這個門不能鎖.

618. The [toilet] is broken.

[tsè-swǒ] hwài le. [廁所]壞了.

619. The room is too [cold] [hot].

jèi-ge fáng-jyān tài [lěng] [rè]. 這個房間太[冷][熱].

620. Is this drinking water?

jèi shr̀ bu-shr̀ yǐn-yùng shwěi? 這是不是飲用水?

621. There is no hot water.
méi-yǒu rè shwěi. 沒有熱水.

622. Spray [for insects] [for vermin].
[kwūn-chúng] [hái-chùng] jì. [昆蟲] [害蟲] 劑.

623. Wash and iron [this shirt].
chǐng bǎ [jèi-jyàn chèn-shān] syǐ gēn tàng.
請把 [這件襯衫] 洗跟燙.

624. Bring me another [blanket].
chǐng lìng-wài gěi wǒ [yì-jāng tǎn-dz].
請另外給我 [一張毯子].

625. Change the sheets.
chǐng bǎ bèi-dār hwàn yí-syà. 請把被單換一下.

626. Make the bed.
chǐng bǎ chwáng jéng-lǐ yí-syà. 請把牀整理一下.

627. A bath mat.
yù-shǐ de jyǎu-dyàn. 浴室的腳墊.

628. A bed sheet. chwáng-dān-dz. 床單子.

629. A candle. là-jú. 蠟燭.

630. Some coathangers. yì-syē yī-jyà. 一些衣架.

631. A pillow. yí-ge jěn-tóu. 一個枕頭.

632. A pillowcase. yí-ge jěn-tàu. 一個枕套.

633. An adaptor for electrical appliances.
dyàn-chì byàn-yā-chì. 電器變壓器.

634. Some soap. yì-syē féi-dzàu. 一些肥皂.

635. Some toilet paper.
yì-syē tsáu-jř. 一些草紙.

636. A towel. máu-jīn.　毛巾.

637. A wash basin.　lyǎn-pén.　臉盆.

RENTING AN APARTMENT

638. I want to rent an apartment [with a bathroom].
wǒ yàu dzū yì-jyān [yǒu yí-ge yù-shř de] gūng-yù.
我要租一間[有一個浴室的]公寓.

639. —with two bedrooms.
—yǒu lyǎng-ge shwèi-fáng de.　—有兩個睡房的.

640. —with a living room.
—yǒu yí-ge kè-tīng de.　—有一個客廳的.

641. —with a dining room.
—yǒu yí-ge fàn-tīng de.　—有一個飯廳的.

642. —with a kitchen.
—yǒu yí-ge chú-fáng de.　—有一個廚房的.

643. A furnished apartment.
yì-jyān yǒu jyā-jyù de gūng-yù.
一間有家具的公寓.

644. An unfurnished apartment.
yì-jyān méi-yǒu jyā-jyù de gūng-yù.
一間沒有家具的公寓

645. Do you furnish [the linen] [the dishes]?
nǐ-men gūng-jǐ [bèi-dān] [dyé-dz] ma?
你們供給[被單][碟子]嗎?

646. —maid service.
—nyǔ-yùng-rén fú-wù.　—女傭人服務

647. Must we sign a lease?
wǒ-men syū-yàu chyān yí-ge dzū-ywē ma?
我們需要簽一個租約嗎?

APARTMENT: USEFUL WORDS

648. Alarm clock. naù-jūng. 鬧鐘.

649. Ashtray. yān-hwēi-dyé. 烟灰碟.

650. Bathtub. dzǎu-pén. 澡盆.

651. Bottle opener. kāi-píng-chì. 開瓶器.

652. Broom. sàu-jou. 掃帚.

653. Can opener. kāi-gwàn-chì. 開罐器.

654. Chair. yǐ-dz. 椅子.

655. Chest of drawers. yī-gwèi. 衣櫃.

656. Closet. yī-chú. 衣櫥.

657. The cook. chú-dz. 廚子.

658. Cork (OR: **Stopper**). sāi-dz. 塞子.

659. Corkscrew. bá-sāi-dzwàn. 拔塞鑽.

660. Curtains (OR: **Drapes**).
chwāng-lyán. 窗簾.

661. Cushion (for chair). yǐ-dyàn. 椅墊.

662. Dishwasher. syí-wǎn-jī. 洗碗机.

663. Doorbell. mén-líng. 門鈴.

664. Dryer. gān-yī-jī. 乾衣机.

665. Fan (**hand-held**). shàn-dz. 扇子.

666. Floor. dì-bǎn. 地板.

667. Hassock. syī-dyàn. 膝墊.

668. Lamp. dēng. 燈.

669. Mirror. jìng-dz. 鏡子.

670. Mosquito net. wén-jàng. 蚊帳.

671. Napkins (cloth). tsān-jīn. 餐巾.

672. Pail. tǔng-dz. 桶子.

673. Rug. dì-tǎn. 地毯.

674. Shower. chūng-dzǎu. 冲澡.

675. Sink. gwàn-syǐ-chàu. 盥洗槽.

676. Switch (light).
dyàn-dēng kāi-gwān. 電燈開關.

677. Table. jwō-dz. 桌子.

678. Tablecloth. jwō-bu. 桌布.

679. Terrace. lyáng-tái. 涼台.

680. Tray. twō-pán. 托盤.

681. Vase. hwā-píng. 花瓶.

682. Venetian blinds.
wēi-ní-sž bái-yè-lyán. 威尼斯百葉簾.

683. Bamboo blinds. dzù lyán. 竹簾.

684. Veranda. láng-dz. 廊子.

685. Washing machine. syǐ-yī-jī. 洗衣机.

686. Whiskbroom. máu-jou. 毛箒.

CAFÉ AND BAR

687. Bartender, I'd like [a drink].
syān-shēng, wǒ yàu [yì-bēi jyǒu].*
先生，我要 [一杯酒].

* See Note, p. 3

688. —a cocktail. —jī-wéi-jyǒu. 鷄尾酒.

689. —a bottle of mineral water [without gas].
—yì-píng [wú-chì] kwàng-chywán shwěi.
一一瓶 [無汽] 礦泉水.

690. —a whiskey [and soda].
—yì-bēi wēi-shr̀-jì jyǒu [gēn sū-dǎ shwěi].
一一杯威士忌酒 [跟蘇打水].

691. —a cognac.
—fá-gwo bái-lán-di jyǒu. 法國白蘭地酒.

692. —a brandy. —bái-lán-di jyǒu. 白蘭地酒.

693. —a liqueur (OR: **after-dinner drink**).
—yì-bēi lyè-jyǒu. 一一杯烈酒.

694. —gin [and tonic].
—dù-sūng-dz jyǒu [gēn jīn-jī-nà shwěi].
一杯松子酒 [跟金雞納水].

695. —rum. —tyán-jyǒu. 一甜酒.

696. —Scotch whiskey.
—sū-gè-lán chǎn wēi-shr̀-jī jyǒu. 蘇格蘭產威士忌酒.

697. —rye whiskey.
—hēi mài wēi-shr̀-jī jyǒu. 黑麥威士忌酒.

698. —bourbon.
—bā-běn wēi-shr̀-jī jyǒu. 巴本威士忌酒.

699. —vodka. —fú-tè-kǎ. 依特卡.

700. —a lemonade.
—níng-méng shwěi. 檸檬水.

701. —a non-alcoholic drink.
—bù hán jyǒu-jīng de yǐn-lyàu. 不含酒精的飲料.

702. —a bottled fruit drink.
—yì-píng gwǒ shwěi. 一瓶果水.

703. —a light [draft] beer.
—yì-bēi dàn de [shēng] pí-jyǒu. 一杯淡的[生]啤酒.

704. —a dark beer. —hēi pí-jyǒu. 黑啤酒.

705. —champagne.
—syāng-bīng jyǒu. 香檳酒.

706. —a glass of sherry.
—yì-bēi sywě-lì jyǒu. 一杯雪利酒.

707. —[red] [white] wine.
—[húng] [bái] pú-táu jyǒu. [紅][白]葡萄酒.

708. Let's have another.
dzài lái yì-bēi. 再來一杯.

709. To your health!
wèi nín jyàn-kāng gān-bēi (OR: jìng nǐ yì-bēi)!
為您健康乾杯(敬您一杯)!

RESTAURANT

710. Can you recommend a good restaurant [for dinner]?
shì-fǒu ké-yi jyè-shàu yí-ge tè-byé hǎu de fàn-gwǎr [chī wǎn-fàn]?
是否可以介紹一個特別好的飯館兒[吃晚飯]?

711. —for a snack. —chī dyǎn-syīn. 一吃點心.

712. Do you serve [lunch]?
shì-fǒu yǒu [jūng-fàn] ké chī? 是否有[中飯]可吃?

713. At what time is [supper] served?
shém-ma shŕ-hòu chŕ [wǎn-fàn]? 什麼時候吃[晚飯]?

714. There are [three] of us.
wǒ-men [sān] wèi. 我們[三]位.

715. Are you my [waiter] [waitress]?
nín shr̀-fǒu wǒ de [shr̀-jě] [nyǔ shr̀-jě]?
您是否我的[侍者][女侍者]?

716. I prefer a table [by the window].
wǒ syǐ-hwān yí-ge [kàu-je chwāng-hù de] jwō-dz.
我喜歡一個[靠著窗戶的]桌子.

717. —in the corner.
—dzài jwán jyáu chù. —在轉角處.

718. —outdoors.   —dzài wài-tóu. —在外頭.

719. —indoors.   —dzài lǐ-tóu. —在裏頭.

720. I'd like to wash my hands.
wǒ syǎng syǐ-yi-syǐ shǒu. 我想洗一洗手.

721. We want to eat lightly.
wǒ-men yàu chŕ yì-dyǎr. 我們要吃一點兒.

722. What is the specialty of the house?
běn gwǎr de tè-byé tsài shr̀ shém-ma?
本館的特別菜是什麼?

723. What kind of [fish] do you have?
nǐ-men yǒu néi-jǔng [yú]? 你們有那種[魚]?

724. Please serve us as quickly as you can.
chǐng kwài dyǎr shàng tsài. 請快點兒上菜.

725. Bring me [the menu].
chǐng gěi wǒ [tsài-dān]. 請給我[菜單].

726. —the wine list. —jyǒu-dān. —酒單.

727. —**water** [**with**] [**without**] **ice.**
—shwĕi [gēn] [bù-gēn] bīng-kwài.
— 水 [跟] [不 跟] 冰 塊 .

728. —**bread.** —myàn-bāu. — 麵 包 .

729. —**butter.** —nǎi-yóu. — 奶 油 .

730. —**chopsticks.** —kwài-dz. — 筷 子 .

731. —**a cup.** —yí-ge chá-bēi. — 一 個 茶 杯 .

732. —**a fork.** —yì-jĭ chā-dz. — 一 支 叉 子 .

733. —**a glass.** —yí-ge shwĕi-bēi. — 一 個 水 杯 .

734. —**a** [**sharp**] **knife.**
—yì-jĭ [lì] dāu. — 一 支 [利] 刀 .

735. —**a plate.** —yí-ge pán-dz. — 一 個 盤 子 .

736. —**a soup spoon.**
—yí-ge tāng-chŕ. — 一 個 湯 匙 .

737. —**a saucer.** —yí-ge chá-dyé. — 一 個 茶 碟 .

738. —**a teaspoon.** —yí-ge chá-chŕ. — 一 個 茶 匙 .

739. I want something [**plain**] [**without meat**].
wŏ yàu [hĕn jyǎn-dān] [méi-yŏu ròu dzài nèi] de.
我 要 [很 簡 單] [沒 有 肉 在 內] 的 .

740. Is it [**canned**]?
shŕ-fŏu [gwàn-tóu de]? 是 否 [罐 頭 的] ?

741. —**fatty** (OR: **greasy**).
—yóu-nì de. — 油 膩 的 .

742. —**fresh.** —syīn-syan de. — 新 鮮 的 .

743. —**frozen.** —dùng de. — 凍 的 .

744. —**lean.** —shòu de. — 瘦 的 .

745. —**peppery.** —là de. - 辣 的.

746. —**salty.** —syán de. - 鹹 的.

747. —**spicy.**
—jyā yǒu syāng lyàu de. - 加有香料的.

748. —**sweet.** —tyán de. - 甜 的.

749. How is it prepared?
jèi-ge dzěm-ma-yàng dzwò de? 這個怎麼樣做的?

750. Is it [baked]? shr̀-fǒu [kǎu de]? 是否[烤]的?

751. —**boiled** (OR: **poached**). —jǔ de. - 煮的.

752. —**braised.** —shāu de. - 燒 的.

753. —**breaded.** —gwó-fěn de. - 裹粉的.

754. —**broiled.** —shāu-kǎu de. - 燒 烤的.

755. —**chopped.** —chyē-syì de. - 切細的.

756. —**deep-fried.** —já de. - 炸的.

757. —**fried.** —yǒu-jyān de. - 油 煎 的.

758. —**grilled.** —shāu de. - 燒 的.

759. —**roasted.** —kǎu de. - 烤 的.

760. —**sautéed.** —nwùn-jyān de. - 嫩 煎 的.

761. —**on a skewer.**
—dzài yí-ge kǎu-ròu-chā de. - 在一個烤肉叉的.

762. —**preserved.** —syán de. - 鹹 的.

763. —**steamed.** —jēng de. - 蒸 的.

764. —**stewed.** —dwùn de. - 燉 的.

765. This is [stale (LIT.: **not fresh)].**
jèi-ge [bu syīn-syan]. 這個[不新鮮].

766. —**too tough.** —tài yìng. - 太 硬.

767. —too dry. —tài gān. 太乾.

768. —too cold. —tài lěng. 太冷.

769. I like the meat [rare].
wǒ syǐ-hwān shāu de [hěn nwùn de] ròu.
我喜歡燒的 [很嫩的] 肉.

770. —medium.
—bàn-shēng shú de. 半生熟的.

771. —well done. —hěn shú de. 很熟的.

772. The dish is [undercooked].
jèi-ge tsài [jǔ de bu-gòu shú]. 這個菜 [煮的不夠熟].

773. —burned. —shāu-jyāu le. 燒焦了.

774. Does it taste like [chicken]?
wèi-dàu shr̀-fǒu gēn [jī] yí-yàng? 味道是否跟 [鷄] 一樣?

775. A little more. dzài jyā yì-dyǎr. 再加一點兒.

776. A little less. shǎu yì-dyǎr. 少一點兒.

777. Something else. chí-tā de. 其他的.

778. A small portion. yì-dyǎr. 一點兒.

779. The next course.
dì-èr-dàu tsài. 第二道菜.

780. I have just enough.
wǒ gāng chī gòu le. 我剛吃夠了.

781. This is [not clean] [dirty].
jèi-ge [bù gān-jìng] [dzāng]. 這個 [不乾淨] [髒].

782. I did not order this.
wǒ méi-yǒu jyàu jèi-ge. 我沒有叫這個.

783. You may take this away.
nǐ kě bǎ jèi-ge ná-dzǒu. 你可把這個拿走.

784. May I change this for [a salad]?

wǒ shr̀-fǒu kě bǎ jèi-ge hwàn [yì-pán shā-là]?

我是否可把這個換 [一盤沙拉]？

785. What flavors do you have (LIT.: **What kinds do you have**)?

nǐ-men yǒu néi-jí-jǔng? 你們有那幾種？

786. The check, please.

chǐng ná jàng-dān lái. 請拿賬單來.

787. Do I pay at the cashier's desk?

wǒ shr̀-fǒu dàu chū-nà-chù fù-jàng? 我是否到出納處付賬？

788. Is the tip included?

syǎu-fèi shr̀-fǒu bāu-kwò dzài nèi? 小費是否包括在內？

789. There is a mistake in the bill.

jàng-dān yǒu tswò-wù. 賬單有錯誤.

790. What are these charges for?

jèi-syē chyán shr̀ gàn-shém-ma de? 這些錢是幹什麼的？

791. The food and service were excellent.

tsài gēn fú-wù dōu dǐng hǎu! 菜跟服務都頂好.

792. Hearty appetite!

wèi-kou jèng hǎu! 胃口正好.

FOOD: SPICES AND SEASONINGS

793. Condiments. dyàu-wèi-pǐn. 調味品

794. Anise seed. hwéi-syāng-dz. 茴香子.

795. Chili paste. là jyàng. 辣醬.

796. Cinnamon. gwèi-pí. 桂皮.

797. Cloves. dīng-syāng. 丁香.

798. Duck (OR: **Plum**) **sauce.**
yā jyàng. 鴨醬.

799. Five perfume spice powder (a blend of star anise, cinnamon, clove, fennel and red pepper).
wǔ-syāng-lyàu. 五香料.

800. Garlic. swàn. 蒜.

801. Ginger. jyāng. 薑.

802. [Hot] [Mild] mustard.
[là de] [bu shì hěn là de] jyē-mwò jyàng.
[辣的] [不是很辣的] 芥末醬.

803. Oyster sauce. háu-yóu. 蠔油.

804. Peanut oil. hwā-shēng-yóu. 花生油.

805. Hot chili peppers. là-jyāu. 辣椒.

806. Black pepper. hú-jyāu. 胡椒.

807. Red pepper. chín-jyāu. 青椒.

808. Szechuan pepper.
sż-chwān hú-jyāu. 四川胡椒.

809. Pepper oil. là-yóu. 辣油.

810. Pickles. swān-syǎu-tsài. 酸小菜.

811. Salt. yán. 鹽.

812. Seasoning powder (OR: **Monosodium glutamate**).
wèi-jīng. 味精.

813. Sesame seeds. jř-má. 芝麻.

814. Sesame seed oil. syāng-yóu. 香油.

815. **Soy sauce.** jyāng-yóu. 醬油.

816. **Sugar.** táng. 糖.

817. **Vinegar.** tsù. 醋.

818. **Wine vinegar.** jèn jyāng tsù. 鎮江醋.

BEVERAGES AND BREAKFAST FOODS

819. **[Black] coffee.** [chwún] kā-fēi. [純] 咖啡.

820. **Coffee [with cream].**
kā-fēi [gēn nǎi-yóu]. 咖啡 [跟奶油].

821. **—with milk.** —gēn nyóu-nǎi. 一跟牛奶.

822. **—with an artificial sweetener.**
—gēn rén-dzàu táng. 一跟人造糖.

823. **Hot chocolate.**
rè de chyǎu-kè-lì yǐn-lyàu. 熱的巧克力飲料.

824. **Tea [with lemon].**
[níng-méng] chá. [檸檬] 茶.

825. **Iced [tea] [coffee].**
bīng [chá] [kā-fēi]. 冰 [茶] [咖啡].

826. **Fruit juice.** gwǒ-jī. 菓汁.

827. **Orange juice.** jyú-dz jēr. 橘子汁.

828. **Tomato juice.** fān-chyé shwěi. 蕃茄水.

829. **Bread.** myàn-bāu. 麵包.

830. Pastry. dyǎn-syīn. 點心

831. Rolls. myàn-bāu jywǎn. 麵包捲

832. Toast. kǎu myàn-bāu. 烤麵包

833. Jam. gwǒ-jyàng. 果醬

834. Marmalade.
jyú-dz gwǒ-dz jyàng. 橘子果子醬

835. [Cooked] [Dry] cereal.
[jǔ de] [gān de] mài-pyàn. [煮的] [乾的] 麥片

836. Pancakes. bwó káu-bǐng. 薄烤餅

837. [Bacon] [Ham] and eggs.
[syán-ròu] [hwó-twěi] gēn jī-dàn.
[燻肉] [火腿] 跟雞蛋

838. [Soft-boiled] [Hard-boiled] eggs.
[bàn-shú de] [chywán-shú de] jī-dàn.
[半熟的] [全熟的] 雞蛋

839. Fried eggs. jyān dàn. 煎蛋

840. Poached eggs. hé-bāu dàn. 荷包蛋

841. Scrambled eggs.
chǎu jī-dàn. 炒雞蛋

842. Omelet. fú-róng dàn. 芙蓉蛋

SOUPS AND SALADS

843. [Beef] broth.
[nyóu-ròu] chīng tāng. [牛肉] 清湯

844. Chicken soup. jī tāng. 雞湯

845. Tomato soup. fān-chyé tāng. 番茄湯

846. **Vegetable soup.** tsài tāng. 菜湯.

847. **Green salad.** chīng-tsài shā-là. 青菜沙拉.

848. **Potato salad.**
mǎ-líng-shǔ shā-là. 馬鈴薯沙拉.

849. **Seafood salad.** hǎi-wèi shā-là. 海味沙拉.

850. **Shrimp salad.** syā-rén shā-là. 蝦仁沙拉.

851. **Tomato salad.** fān-chyé shā-là. 蕃茄沙拉.

852. **Salad dressing.** shā-là jyàng. 沙拉醬.

MEATS

853. **[Roast] [Ground] beef.**
[kǎu] [jǎn-swèi de] nyóu-ròu. [烤] [碾碎的] 牛肉.

854. **Beefsteak.** nyóu-pái. 牛排.

855. **Brains.** nǎu-dz. 腦子.

856. **Chops.** pái-gǔ ròu. 排骨肉.

857. **Cutlets.** ròu-pyàn. 肉片.

858. **Game.** yě-wèi. 野味.

859. **Heart.** syīn-dzàng. 心臟.

860. **Kidneys.** yāu-dz. 腰子.

861. **Lamb.** syǎu-yáng-ròu. 小羊肉.

862. **(Calves') liver.** (syǎu-nyóu)-gān. (小牛)肝.

863. **Meatballs.** ròu wán. 肉丸.

864. **Meatloaf.** swèi ròu kwài. 碎肉塊.

865. **Mutton.** yáng-ròu. 羊肉.

866. **Pork.** jū-ròu. 豬肉.
867. **Sausage.** là-cháng. 臘腸
868. **Tongue.** shé-tóu. 舌頭.
869. **Veal.** syǎu-nyóu-ròu. 小牛肉.
870. **Venison.** lù-ròu. 鹿肉.

POULTRY

871. **Chicken.** jī. 雞
872. **Duck.** yā-dz. 鴨子.
873. **Goose.** é. 鵝
874. **Pigeon.** gē-dz. 鴿子
875. **Squab.** rǔ-gē. 乳鴿
876. **Turkey.** hwǒ-jī. 火雞

FISH AND SEAFOOD

877. **Abalone.** bāu-yú. 鮑魚.
878. **Bass.** lú-yú. 鱸魚.
879. **Carp.** lǐ-yú. 鯉魚.
880. **Clams.** gě. 蛤
881. **Cod.** sywě-yú. 鱈魚.
882. **Crab.** páng-syè. 螃蟹
883. **Crayfish.** áu-syā. 螯蝦

884. Cuttlefish. yóu-yú. 魷魚.

885. Eel. màn-yú. 鰻魚.

886. Halibut. dà-bǐ-mù-yú. 大比目魚

887. Herring. chīng-yú. 青魚

888. Jellyfish. hái jè pí. 海蜇片

889. Lobster. lúng-syā. 龍蝦

890. Mackerel. chīng-yú. 青魚

891. Mussels. yí-bèi. 貽貝

892. Oysters. háu. 蠔

893. Perch. jì-yú. 鯽魚

894. Prawns. dà-syār. 大蝦

895. Salmon. sà-mén-yú. 薩門魚.

896. Sardine. shā-dīng-yú. 沙丁魚

897. Scallops. shàn-bèi-ké. 扇貝壳

898. Sea cucumber. hǎi-shēn. 海參

899. Shark's fin. yú-chì. 魚翅

900. Shrimp. syǎu-syār. 小蝦

901. Snails. gwā-nyóu. 蝸牛

902. Sole. tǎ-yú. 鰨魚

903. Squid. yǒu-yú. 魷魚.

904. Sturgeon. hwáng-yú. 黃魚

905. Swordfish. chí-yú. 旗魚

906. Trout. jwǔn-yú. 鱒魚

907. Tuna. wěi. 鮪

908. Turbot. píng-yú. 平魚.

VEGETABLES

909. Artichoke. chǎu-syán-jì. 朝鮮劍.

910. Asparagus. lú-swǔn. 芦筍.

911. Bamboo shoots. jú-swǔn. 竹筍.

912. Beans. dòu. 豆.

913. Bean sprouts. dòu-yá-tsài. 豆芽菜.

914. Beets. húng-tsài-tóu. 紅菜豆.

915. Bitter melon. kǔ-gwā. 苦瓜.

916. Black beans. hēi-dòu. 黑豆.

917. Cabbage. yáng-bái-tsài. 洋白菜.

918. Chinese cabbage. bái-tsài. 白菜.

919. Carrots. húng-lwó-bwō. 紅蘿卜.

920. Cauliflower. yáng-tsài-hwār. 洋菜花.

921. Celery. chín-tsài. 芹菜.

922. Corn. yù-mǐ. 玉米.

923. Cucumber. hwáng-gwā. 黄瓜.

924. Eggplant. chyé-dz. 茄子.

925. Horseradish. là-gēn. 辣根.

926. Kidney beans. yāu-dòu. 腰豆.

927. Leeks. yǒu-tsài. 油菜.

928. Lettuce. shēng-tsài. 生菜.

929. Lima beans. tsán-dòu. 蚕豆.

930. Lotus root. ǒu. 藕.

931. Mushrooms. dūng-gǔ. 冬菇.

932. Okra. chyōu-kwéi. 秋葵.

933. Olives. gán-lǎn. 甘欖.

934. Onions. yáng-tsūng. 洋葱.

935. Parsley. syāng-tsài. 香菜.

936. Chinese parsley. ywán-shwēi. 芫荽.

937. Peas. wān-dòu. 碗豆.

938. Green peppers. chīng-jyāu. 青椒.

939. Potatoes. mǎ-líng-shǔ. 馬鈴薯.

940. Pumpkin. nán-gwá. 南瓜.

941. Radish. húng-syí-lwó-bwō. 紅須蘿卜.

942. Rhubarb. dà-hwáng. 大黄.

943. Snow peas. sywě-dòu. 雪豆.

944. Soybeans. hwáng-dòu. 黄豆.

945. Soybean curd. dòu-fú. 豆腐.

946. Spinach. bwō-tsài. 溌菜.

947. Squash. gwā. 瓜.

948. Sweet potatoes. bái-shǔ. 白薯.

949. Tomatoes. fān-chyé. 番茄.

950. Turnips. bái-lwó-bwō. 白蘿卜.

951. Water chestnut. má-tí. 馬蹄.

952. Winter melon. dūng-gwā. 冬瓜.

GRAINS, CEREALS AND STARCHES

953. Barley. dà-mài. 大麥.

954. Bran. kāng. 糠.

955. Bread (Western). myàn-bàu. 麵包.

956. Bread (Chinese steamed).
mán-tóu. 饅頭.

957. Bread (Chinese round, flat, baked).
bǐng. 餅.

958. Buckwheat. chyáu-mài. 蕎麥.

959. Cornmeal. yù-mǐ-myàr. 玉米麵兒.

960. Dumplings (boiled). jyǎu-dz. 餃子.

961. Dumplings (steamed). bāu-dz. 飽子.

962. Flour. myàn-fěn. 麵粉.

963. Macaroni (OR: Noodles).
gwà-myàn (OR: myàn-tyáu). 掛麵 (麵條).

964. Millet. gǔ-dz. 穀子.

965. Oatmeal. yóu-mài-yàn. 油麥燕.

966. Oats. chywè-mài (OR: yān-mài). 雀麥 (燕麥).

967. Wheat. mài-dz (OR: syǎu-mài). 麥子 (小麥).

968. Rice (uncooked). mǐ. 米.

969. Rice (cooked). fàn. 飯.

FRUITS AND NUTS

970. Almonds. syìng-rén. 杏仁.

971. Apple. píng-gwǒ. 蘋果.

972. Apricot. syìng-dz. 杏子.

973. Banana. syāng-jyāu. 香蕉 .

974. Cantaloupe. tyán-gwā.* 甜瓜 .

975. Cashews. yāu-gwǒ. 腰果 .

976. Cherries. yīng-táu. 櫻桃 .

977. Chestnut. lì-dz. 栗子 .

978. Coconut. yé-dz. 椰子 .

979. Dates. dzǎu-dz. 棗子 .

980. Dried fruit. gān gwǒ-dz. 乾果子 .

981. Figs. wú-hwā-gwǒ. 無花果 .

982. Grapes. pú-táu. 葡萄 .

983. Kumquats. jīn-jú. 金橘 .

984. Lemon. níng-méng. 檸檬 .

985. Lichee. lì-jř. 荔枝 .

986. Lime. bái-gwǒ. 白果 .

987. Longon (dragon eye).
lúng-yán. 龍眼 .

988. Loquats. pí-pá. 枇杷 .

989. Lotus seeds. lyán-dz. 蓮子 .

990. Mandarin orange. mì-gān. 蜜柑 .

991. Mango. máng-gwǒ. 芒果 .

992. Orange. jyú-dz. 橘子 .

993. Peach. táu-dz. 桃子 .

994. Peanuts. hwā-shēng. 花生 .

995. Pear. lí-dz. 梨子 .

* This word can be used for melon in general.

996. Persimmon. shr̀-dz. 柿子.

997. Pineapple. bwō-lwó. 波羅.

998. Plums. lǐ-dz. 李子.

999. Prunes. méi-dz. 梅子.

1000. Pumelo. yòu-dz. 柚子.

1001. Raisins. pú-táu-kàn. 葡萄乾.

1002. Strawberries. tsǎu-méi. 草梅.

1003. Tangerine. jyú-dz. 橘子.

1004. Walnuts. hé-táu. 核桃.

1005. Watermelon. syī-gwā. 西瓜.

DESSERTS

1006. Cake. gāu-dyǎn. 糕點.

1007. Candy. táng-dz. 糖子.

1008. Cookies. bǐng-gān. 餅乾.

1009. Custard. dàn-bù-dīng. 蛋布丁.

1010. Fresh fruit. syīn gwǒ-dz. 新果子.

1011. [Vanilla] [Chocolate] ice cream.
[syāng-tsǎu] [chyǎu-kè-lì] bīng-jī-líng.
[香草][巧克力]冰淇淋

1012. Pie. syàn-bǐng. 餡餅.

1013. Pudding. bù-dīng. 布丁.

1014. Sherbet. bīng-gwǒ-dz-lù. 冰果子露.

CHINESE FOOD

APPETIZERS AND TEA SNACKS*

1015. [Ròu] [Lyán-dz] [Dòu-shā] bāu. [肉] [蓮myō] [莲sha] 包
[Pork] [Sweet lotus-seed jam] [Black bean jam] filled,
   steamed buns.

1016. Chwūn-jywǎn. 春卷.
Spring roll.

1017. Gwō-tyē. 鍋貼.
Fried, pork-filled dumplings.

1018. Háu-yóu mwó-gǔ. 蠔油磨菇.
Fresh mushrooms braised in oyster sauce.

1019. Béi-jīng jyǎu-dz. 北京餃子.
Dumplings in Peking-style sauce (sweet and spicy sauce
   made of soybeans, spices, garlic and chili).

1020. Sż-chwān jyǎu-dz. 西川餃子.
Dumplings in Szechuan-style sauce (chili and peanut oil
   sauce).

1021. Jyǒu-jī. 酒雞.
Drunken chicken (marinated in sherry, sesame oil and soy
   sauce, served cold).

1022. Kǎu pái-gǔ. 烤排骨.
Barbecued spareribs.

---

* The following sections (pp. 70–77) form a list containing the
names and descriptions of some typical food and drink specialties.
While it does not claim to be comprehensive, it is hoped it will
encourage the users of this book to sample the varied and out-
standing cuisines of China. For ease of reference, the Chinese name
is given first, then the English equivalent.

1023. Mì rwǎn-jī. 蜜軟雞.
Boneless cold chicken in honey-oyster sauce.

1024. Syán-dàn. 鹹蛋.
Salted, preserved eggs.

1025. Syār tǔ-sz̄. 蝦土司.
Shrimp toast.

1026. Hwún-dwùn. Won-ton. 餛飩.

SOUPS

1027. Bā bǎu dūng-gwā tāng. 八寶冬瓜湯.
Eight treasure winter melon soup (stock and meat, vegetables steamed and served in the hollowed-out shell of the melon).

1028. Bái-yú tāng. 白玉湯.
White jade soup (with bean sprouts, bean curd, bamboo shoots, mushrooms and chicken broth).

1029. Chīng-tāng syār-chyóu. 清湯蝦球.
Clear broth with ham and shrimp dumplings.

1030. Dàn hwā tāng. 蛋花湯.
Egg drop soup.

1031. Dòu-fú chīng-tsài tāng. 豆腐青菜湯.
Soybean curd and vegetable soup.

1032. Jīn twěi yú dǔ tāng. 金腿魚肚湯.
Golden ham and fish stomach soup.

1033. Jī ěr yān wō tāng. 雞茸燕窩湯.
Bird's nest soup (chicken stock, chicken and mushrooms simmered with cleaned, dried swallow's nest).

1034. Nyóu-ròu bái-tsài tāng. 牛肉白菜湯.
Beef and cabbage soup.

1035. Nyóu-ròu tāng. 牛肉湯.
Beef soup with scallions and ginger.

1036. Swān là tāng. 酸辣湯.

Hot and sour soup (stock simmered with sherry, vinegar, soy sauce and meat or vegetables).

1037. Syè ròu shēng chř tāng. 蟹肉生翅湯.

Crab meat shark's fin soup.

MEAT ENTREES

1038. Chā shāu. 义燒.

Barbecued pork.

1039. Fěn jēng yáng-ròu. 粉蒸羊肉.

Flour-steamed lamb (in casserole with ground rice).

1040. Tyán swān gú lǎu ròu. 甜酸古老肉.

Ancient well-cooked pork (braised with bamboo shoots, green peppers and sweet-sour sauce).

1041. Gwǒ-pí ròu. 果皮肉.

Pork braised with orange rind.

1042. Háu-yóu nyóu-ròu. 蠔油牛肉.

Beef braised in oyster sauce.

1043. Hwó-twěi jywán. 火腿卷.

Ham rolls (with chicken and walnut filling, mushroom and bamboo shoot sauce).

1044. Méng-gú-kǎu yáng. 蒙古烤羊.

Mongolian lamb and scallions.

1045. Mù-syū ròu gēn bwó-bíng. 木須肉跟薄餅.

Moo shoo pork with Peking doilies.

1046. Shř-dz tóu. 獅子頭.

Lion's head (large meatballs made of minced pork, fried with cabbage and stewed for several hours).

1047. Syān-swǔn mwó-gǔ nyóu-ròu.
鮮筍蘑菇牛肉.
Beef braised with bamboo shoots and mushrooms.

1048. Syŭn nyóu-ròu. 燻中肉.
Smoked beef (with fragrant spices).

1049. Sywĕ-dòu cháu nyóu-ròu. 雪豆炒牛肉.
Stir-fried beef and snow peas.

1050. Sż-chwān jū-ròu. 四川銘肉.
Twice-cooked pork, Szechuan style.

1051. Tyè shù bá nyóu. 鐵樹扒中.
Chinese steaks.

1052. Wŭ-syāng pái-gŭ. 五香排骨.
Five fragrance spareribs (marinated with soy sauce, wine,
   cloves, cinnamon, anise seed powder and mustard).

POULTRY ENTREES

1053. Béi-jīng yā. 北京鴨.
Peking duck.

1054. Fān-shú chău syāng-yā. 蕃薯炒香鴨.
Fragrant duck braised with sweet potatoes.

1055. Jēng rŭ-gē dwūn yàn wō. 蒸乳鴿燉燕窩.
Steamed squab stuffed with bird's nest.

1056. Jēng syī-gwā yā. 蒸西瓜鴨.
Boneless duck steamed in whole watermelon with mushrooms.

1057. Jyǒu-jēng chywán yā. 酒蒸全鴨.
Whole duckling steamed in white wine.

1058. Níng-méng rwăn-jī. 檸檬軟鷄.
Boneless chicken in lemon sauce.

1059. Sywĕ-lí chău-jī. 雪梨炒鷄.
Snow pear cooked chicken (shredded chicken braised with
   sliced pears).

1060. Tswèi-pí jī. 脆皮鷄.
Deep-fried paper-wrapped chicken.

1061. Wǔ-syāng jī. 五香鷄

Five fragrance chicken (barbecued in cinnamon, cloves
aniseed and ginger powder).

FISH AND SEAFOOD ENTREES

1062. Bái-tsài bai yú-ywán. 白菜白魚圓

Braised Chinese cabbage over fish croquettes.

1063. Bàn míng-há. 伴明蝦

Mixed shrimps poached with egg and mustard sauce.

1064. Chǎu syā-rén. 炒蝦仁

Sautéed jumbo shrimp.

1065. Chīng-tsài já yú chyóu. 青菜炸魚球

Deep-fried fish balls and vegetables.

1066. Gwǎng-dūng lúng-syār hú. 廣東龍蝦餬

Lobster Cantonese.

1067. Húng-shāu lǐ-yú. 紅燒鯉魚

Red-cooked carp (simmered in soy sauce).

1068. Lú-shwǔn bāu-yú mèn jī. 蘆荀鮑魚燜鷄

Stir-fried abalone with chicken and asparagus.

1069. Sž-chwān já yú chyóu. 四川炸魚球

Deep-fried fish squares, Szechuan style.

1070. Tyán swān yú. 甜酸魚

Sweet and sour fish (in vinegar and sugar sauce).

VEGETABLE AND EGG ENTREES

1071. Chǎu bái-tsài. 炒白菜

Sautéed cabbage (with soy sauce, ginger, scallions, meat,
fish or bean curd).

1072. Chǎu dòu-fú. 炒豆腐

Fried bean curd.

1073. Chǎu chyé-dz. 炒茄子.

Stir-fried fragrant eggplant (deep-fried eggplant cubes sautéed with meat, vegetables, mushrooms, soy sauce and sherry and garnished with chopped nuts).

1074. Fú-rǔng dàn. 芙蓉蛋.

Deep-fried egg foo yung (omelet fried with chopped meat, seafood or vegetables).

1075. Lwó hàn dzài. 羅漢齊.

Buddha's vegetable dish (mixed fresh and dried vegetables, nuts and mushrooms sautéed in soy sauce and sherry).

1076. Yā-sz dàn-jywǎn. 鴨絲蛋捲.

Steamed omelet rolls with minced duck filling.

NOODLE AND RICE ENTREES

1077. Chǎu-fàn. 炒飯.

Fried rice.

1078. Chǎu-myàn. 炒麵.

Fried noodles.

1079. Já-jyàng myàn. 炸醬麵.

Noodles with sauce.

1080. Jū-ròu chǎu-myàn. 豬肉炒麵.

Noodles with pork.

1081. Làu-myàn. 撈麵.

Parboiled noodles.

1082. Lwó hàn jōu. 羅漢粥.

Buddha congee (rice gruel simmered with chicken stock and dried seafood).

1083. Shř jín gwō bā. 十錦鍋巴.

Sizzling rice crusts with shrimp sauce.

DESSERTS AND SWEETS

1084. Béi-jīng fén. 北京粉.
Peking dust (chestnut puree with sugar, cream and vanilla, topped with whipped cream and preserved fruit).

1085. Jr̄-má bǐng. 芝麻餅.
Sesame seed cookies.

1086. Syìng-rén dòu-fú. 杏仁豆腐.
Almond jelly.

1087. Tyán chéng chá. 甜橙茶.
Sweet orange tea (fresh oranges boiled with sugar, water and rice flour).

TEAS

1088. Húng chá. 紅茶.
Red (common black) tea.

1089. Lúng jǐng chá. 龍井茶.
Dragon's well tea (finest green tea).

1090. Mù li chá. 茉莉茶.
Jasmine tea.

1091. Tyě gwān-yīn chá. 鐵觀音茶.
Iron goddess of mercy tea (black and fragrant).

1092. Wū lúng chá. 烏龍茶.
Black dragon tea (oo long).

CHINESE LIQUORS

1093. Shàu-syīng jyǒu. 紹興酒.
Shao-shing yellow wine (made from rice, used for drinking and cooking, similar to sherry).

1094. Gāu-lyáng jyŏu. 高粱酒.
Kao-ling wine (made from sorghum, clear and potent,
    drunk as liqueur after meals).

1095. Méi-gwèi jyŏu. 玫瑰酒.
Rose-petal wine (fragrant, rose-petal flavored, potent).

1096. Mí jyŏu. 米酒.
Rice wine.

HOLIDAYS

1097. New Year.
syīn nyán. 新年.

1098. A public holiday.
gūng-gùng jyǎ-r̀. 公共假日.

1099. Christmas. shèng-dàn. 聖誕.

1100. Easter. fù-hwó-jyé. 復活節.

1101. Dragon boat festival.*
dwàn-wǔ-jyè. 端午節.

1102. Mid-Autumn festival.†
jǔng-chyōu-jyè. 中秋節.

1103. Day of death.‡
chīng-míng-shǎu-mū. 清明掃墓.

1104. Spring festival.§ chūn-jyè. 春節.

---

    * The beginning of the sunny season—features dragon boat races
and rice cakes wrapped in bamboo leaves.
    † A gathering to look at the full moon and eat moon cakes.
    ‡ A time for honoring dead ancestors and cleaning their graves,
on March 15.
    § Three-day holiday beginning January 1 celebrated with family
activities and fireworks.

SIGHTSEEING

1105. I want a licensed guide [who speaks English].

wǒ yàu yí-ge [hwèi shwō yīng-yǔ] yǒu jŕ-jàu de dǎu-yóu.

我要一個[會説英語]有執照的導遊。

1106. How long will the excursion take?

lyǔ-syíng syū-yàu dwō-shau shŕ-jyān?

旅行需要多少時間？

1107. Must I book in advance?

wǒ shŕ-fǒu syū-yàu yù-syān dēng-jì?

我是否需要預先登記？

1108. Are admission tickets and lunch included?

rù-chǎng pyàu gēn wǔ-tsān dōu jyā shàng ma?

入場票跟午餐都加上嗎？

1109. What is the charge for a trip [to the island]?

[dàu nèi-ge dǎu de] lyǔ-syíng syū-yàu dwō-shau chyán?

[到那個島的]旅行需要多少錢？

1110. —to the mountain.

—dàu shān shàng de. 一 到 山上的.

1111. —to the seashore.

—dàu hǎi-byār de. 一 到 海邊的.

1112. —around the city.

jōu-yóu shŕ nèi de. 一周遊市内的.

1113. —to the suburbs (OR: **environs**).

—dàu jyāu wài de. 一 到 郊外的.

1114. Call for me [tomorrow] at my hotel at 8 A.M.

chǐng [míng-tyān] dzǎu-shàng bā-dyǎn-jūng dàu wǒ de lyú-gwǎn lái-jyē wǒ.

請[明天]早上八點鐘到我的旅館來接我.

1115. Show me the interesting sights.

chǐng dài wǒ chyù kàn-kàn yǒu syìng-chyù de dì-fāng.

請帶我去看看有興趣的地方.

1116. What is [that building]?
[nèi-ge gāu-lóu] jyàu shém-ma? [那個高樓] 叫什麼?

1117. How old is it (LIT.: **How long ago was it built**)?
jyàn le dwō-jyòu le? 建了多久了?

1118. Can we go in?
wǒ-men shr̀-fǒu ké-yi jìn-chyù? 我們是否可以進去?

1119. I am interested in [architecture].
wǒ dwèi [jyàn-jù] tè-byé yǒu syìng-chyù.
我對[建築]特別有興趣.

1120. —archeology. káu-gǔ-swyé. —考古學.

1121. —sculpture. —dyāu-kè-shù. —彫刻術.

1122. —painting. —hwà-hwàr. —畫畫兒.

1123. —graphic art.
—tú-àn yì-shù. —圖案藝術.

1124. —native arts and crafts.
—běn-dì yì-shù hé gūng-yì. —本地藝術和工藝

1125. —modern art.
—syàn-dài yì-shù. —現代藝術.

1126. I should like to see [the park].
wǒ syǎng kàn-kàn [gūng-ywán]. 我想看看[公園].

1127. —the cathedral.
—dà jyàu-táng. —大教堂.

1128. —the business district.
—shr̀-chyū. —市區.

1129. —the caves. —dùng sywè. —洞穴.

1130. —the library.
—tú-shū-gwǎn. —圖書館.

1131. —the ruins. —gǔ-jì. —古蹟.

1132. —**the Great Wall.**
—wàn lí cháng chéng.　萬里長城.

1133. —**the castle.**　—chéng bǎu.　-城堡.

1134. —**the pagoda.**　—báu tǎ. - 宝塔.

1135. —**the palace.**　—gūng-dyàn.-宮殿.

1136. —**the temple.**　—shŕ myàu. - 寺廟.

1137. —**the tomb.**　—mù-líng. - 墓陵.

1138. —**the zoo.**　—dùng-wù-ywán. - 動物園.

1139. Let's take a walk around [the botanical garden].
wǒ-men dàu [jŕ-wù-ywán] dzǒu-yi-dzǒu.
我們到[植物園]走一走.

1140. Is it a tourist trap?
jŕ-shŕ pyàn-pyàn yǒu-kè de dì-fāng ma?
只是騙騙遊客的地方嗎?

1141. A beautiful view!
fēng-jǐng hǎu pyàu-lyàng. 風景好漂亮!

1142. Very interesting!
hěn yǒu yì-sż. 很有意思.

1143. Magnificent!
táng hwáng jí le! 堂皇極了!

1144. We are enjoying ourselves.
wǒ-men wán de hěn syìng-fèn! 我們玩得很興奮!

1145. I am bored.　wǒ hěn wú-lyáu. 我很無聊.

1146. When does the museum [open] [close]?
jèi-ge bwó-wù-gwǎn shém-ma shŕ-hòu [kāi] [gwān]?
這個博物館什麼時候[開][關]?

1147. Is this the way to [the entrance] [the exit]?
dàu [dà-mén-kǒu] [chū-kǒu] shŕ-fǒu tsúng jèi-byān dzǒu?
到[大門口][出口]是否從這邊走?

1148. Let's visit the fine arts gallery.
wǒ-men chyù tsān-gwān nèi-ge měi-shù-gwǎn ba.
我們去參觀那個美術館吧.

1149. Let's stay longer.
wǒ-men dwō dāi yì-hwěr ba. 我們多待一會兒吧.

1150. Let's leave now.
wǒ-men syàn-dzài dzǒu ba. 我們現在走吧.

1151. We must be back by 5 o'clock.
wǒ-men děi wú-dyǎn hwéi-chyù. 我們得五點回去.

1152. If there is time, let's rest a while.
yǒu kùng de hwà, wǒ-men syōu-syi yì-hwěr ba!
有空的話,我們休息一會兒吧!

WORSHIP

1153. Altar. jì-tán. 祭壇.

1154. Catholic church.
tyān-jǔ jyàu-táng. 天主教堂.

1155. Choral music. jàn-měi-shī. 讚美詩.

1156. Collection plate.
mù-jywān-pán. 募捐盤.

1157. Communion. shèng tsān. 聖餐.

1158. Confession. mì-mì tsán-kwèi. 祕密懺悔.

1159. Contribution. jywān jèng. 捐贈.

1160. Mass. mí-sǎ. 彌撒.

1161. Minister. mù-shī. 牧師.

1162. Prayers. chí-dǎu. 祈禱.

1163. Prayer book. chí-dǎu shū. 祈禱書.

1164. Priest. chwán-jyàu-shr̀. 傳教士.

1165. Protestant church.
jī-dū jyàu-táng. 基督教堂.

1166. Rabbi. yóu-tài jyàu shén-fu. 猶太教神父.

1167. Sermon. jyǎng dàu. 講道.

1168. Services. lǐ-bài shr̀. 禮拜式.

1169. Sunday (OR: **Church) school.**
jǔ-r̀-sywé. 主日學

1170. Synagogue.
yóu-tài rén hwèi-táng. 猶太人會堂.

1171. Buddhist monk. hé-shàng. 和尚.

1172. Buddhist temple. sz̀. 寺.

1173. A Buddhist. fwó-jyàu-tú. 佛教徒.

1174. Confucian temple. kúng-myàu. 孔廟.

1175. Taoist priest. dàu shr̀. 道士.

1176. Taoist temple. gwàn. 觀.

ENTERTAINMENTS

1177. Is there [a matinée] today?
jīn-tyān shr̀-fǒu yǒu [r̀-syì]? 今天是否有[日戲]?

1178. Has [the show] begun?
[yǎn-syì] kāi-shr̀ le méi-yǒu? [演戲]開始了沒有?

1179. What is playing now?

syàn-dzài yăn shém-ma? 現在演什麼？

1180. Have you any seats for tonight?

jīn-tyān wăn-shàng yŏu méi-yŏu dzwò-wèi?

今天晚上有沒有座位？

1181. How much is [an orchestra seat]?

[jèng tīng chyán păi] dwō-shau chyán? [正廳前排]多少戲？

1182. —a balcony seat.

—lóu-shàng dzwò-wèi. —樓上座位.

1183. —a box.

—bāu-syāng de dzwò-wèi. —包廂的座位.

1184. —a seat in the mezzanine.

—jūng tséng lóu de dzwò-wèi. —中層樓的座位.

1185. Not too far from the stage.

lí tái-shàng bù tài ywăn. 離台上方太遠.

1186. Here is my stub.

wŏ de tswún-gēn dzài jèr. 我的存根在這兒.

1187. Can I see and hear clearly from there?

tsúng nèi-yì-byăr wŏ néng gòu kàn de tīng de chīng-chu ma? 從那一邊兒我能夠看的聽的清楚嗎？

1188. How much should one tip [the usher]?

wŏ-men syū-yàu gĕi [dài-wèi-ywán] dwō-shau syău-fèi? 我們需要給[帶位員]多少小費？

1189. Is smoking permitted here?

wŏ-men shì-fŏu ké-yi dzài jèr chōu-yān? 我們是否可以在這兒抽煙？

1190. How long is the intermission?

jūng-jyān syōu-syi dwō cháng shŕ-jyān? 中間休息多長時間？

1191. When does the show [begin] [end]?

yăn-syì shém-ma shŕ-hòu [kāi-shŕ] [wán-bì]? 演戲什麼時候[開始][完畢]？

1192. Everyone enjoyed the show.
wǒ-men dà-jyā dōu syīn-shǎng jèi-chū syì.
我們大家都欣賞這齣戲.

1193. The ballet. bā-léi-wǔ. 芭蕾舞.

1194. The box office. shòu-pyàu shř. 售票室.

1195. The circus. mǎ-syì chǎng. 馬戲場.

1196. The concert. yīn-ywè hwèi. 音樂會.

1197. The folk dances. tǔ-fēng-wǔ. 土風舞.

1198. The gambling casino.
dǔ-bwó gwǎn. 賭博館.

1199. The [beginning] [end] of the line.
pǎi dwèi de [chí-dyǎn] [jūng-dyǎn].
排隊的[起點][終點].

1200. The movies. dyàn-yǐng. 電影.

1201. The musical comedy.
gēr-wǔ syǐ-jyù. 歌舞喜劇.

1202. The nightclub. yè-dzǔng hwèi. 夜總會.

1203. The opera. gēr-jyù. 歌劇.

1204. The opera glasses.
kàn syì yùng de wàng-ywǎn-jìng. 看戲用的望遠鏡.

1205. The opera house. gēr-jyù ywàn. 歌劇院.

1206. The program.
yǎn-dzàu jyé-mù. 演奏節目.

1207. The puppet show.
gwēi-lěi syì. 傀儡戲.

1208. The reserved seat. yù-dìng syí. 預定席.

1209. The sports event.
yùn-dùng bǐ-sài. 運動比賽.

1210. Standing room. lì-kàn syí-wèi. 立看席位.

1211. The theater. syì-ywàn. 戲院.

1212. The variety show. dzá-shwǎ. 雜耍.

NIGHTCLUB AND DANCING

1213. How much is [the admission charge]?
[rù-chǎng jywàn] dwō-shau chyán? [入場卷]多少錢?

1214. —the cover charge.
—jī-běn fèi-yùng. 基本費用.

1215. —the minimum charge.
—dzwèi dī fèi-yùng. 最低費用.

1216. Is there a floor show?
yǒu méi-yǒu yú-syìng byáu-yǎn? 有没有餘興表演?

1217. Where can we go to dance?
wǒ-men ké-yi dàu nǎr chyù tyàu-wǔ? 我們可以到那兒去跳舞?

1218. May I have this dance?
wǒ ké-yi gēn nín tyàu jèi-yì-jř wǔ ma? 我可以跟您跳這一支舞嗎?

1219. You dance very well.
nín tyàu de hǎu jí le! 您跳的好極了!

1220. Will you play [a fox trot]?
nín kě bu ké-yi tán [hú-bù-wǔ]? 您可不可以彈[狐步舞]?

1221. —a rumba. —lwún-bā-wǔ. 倫巴舞.

1222. —a samba. —shān-bā-wǔ. 珊巴舞.

1223. —a tango. —tàn-gō-wǔ. 探戈舞.

1224. —a waltz. —hwá-ěr-dž-wǔ. 華尔滋舞.

1225. —rock music. —yáu gwǔn ywè. 搖滾樂.

SPORTS AND GAMES

1226. We want to play [soccer].
wǒ-men yàu wán [dzú-chyóu]. 我們要玩[足球].

1227. —basketball. —lán-chyóu. - 籃球.

1228. —cards. —jř-pái. - 紙牌.

1229. —golf. —gāu-ěr-fū-chyóu. - 高尔夫球.

1230. —ping-pong.
—jwō-chyóu (OR: bīng-bōng chyóu).
一桌球 (乒乓球).

1231. —tennis. —wǎng-chyóu. - 網球.

1232. —volleyball. —pái-chyóu. - 排球.

1233. Do you play [chess]?
nǐ syà [syàng-chí] ma? 你下[象棋]嗎?

1234. —checkers. —chí. - 棋.

1235. —go. —wéi-chí. - 圍棋.

1236. Do you play [bridge]?
nǐ dǎ [chyáu-pái] ma? 你打[橋牌]嗎?

1237. —mahjong. —má-chyè. - 馬雀.

1238. Let's go swimming.
wǒ-men chyù yóu-yǔng ba! 我們去游泳吧!

1239. Let's go to [the swimming pool].
wǒ-men dàu [yóu-yǔng-chí] chyù ba!
我們到[游泳池]去吧!

1240. —the beach. —hǎi tān. - 海灘.

1241. —the horse races. —sài mǎ. - 賽馬.

1242. I need [golf equipment].

wǒ syū-yàu [gāu-ěr-fū-chyóu de yùng-jyù].

我 需要 [高爾夫球的用具].

1243. —fishing tackle. —dyàu jyù. —釣具.

1244. —a tennis racket.
—wǎng-chyóu pāi. —網球拍.

1245. Can we go [fishing]?

wǒ-men shr̀-fǒu ké-yi chyù [dyàu yú]?

我們是否可以去[釣魚]?

1246. —horseback riding.
—chí mǎ. —騎馬.

1247. —roller skating.
—hwá lwǔn. —滑輪.

1248. —ice skating. —hwá bīng. —滑冰.

1249. —sledding. —wán sywě chyàu. —玩雪撬.

1250. —skiing. —hwá sywě. —滑雪.

HIKING AND CAMPING

1251. How long a walk is it to the youth hostel?

dàu syǎu-fàn-dyàn yàu dzǒu dwō jyǒu?

到小飯店要走多久?

1252. Are sanitary facilities available?

yǒu méi-yǒu wèi-shēng shè-bei? 有沒有衛生設備?

1253. Campsite. lù-yíng dì. 露營地.

1254. Camping [equipment] [permit].

lù-yíng [yùng-jyù] [syú-kě-jèng]. 露營 [用具] [許可證].

1255. Cooking utensils. chwēi jyù. 炊具.

1256. Footpath. bù dàu. 步道.

1257. Hike. tú-bù lyǔ-syíng. 徒步旅行.

1258. Matches. hwǒ-chái. 火柴.

1259. Picnic. yě-tsān. 野餐.

1260. Rubbish [receptacle].
lā-jī [tǔng]. 垃圾 [桶].

1261. Shortcut. jìn-lù. 近路.

1262. Tent. jàng-peng. 帳篷.

1263. Thermos. nwán shwěi-píng. 暖水瓶.

1264. Drinking water.
yǐn-yùng shwěi. 飲用水.

1265. Firewood. pǐ-chái. 劈柴.

1266. Forest. sēn-lín. 森林.

1267. Lake. hú. 湖.

1268. Mountain. shān. 山.

1269. River. hé. 河.

1270. Stream. syǎu hé. 小河.

BANK AND MONEY

1271. Where can I change foreign money [at the best rate]?
shém-ma dì-fāng wǒ néng [yǐ dzwèi hǎu bǐ hwèi-lyù] hwàn wài-gwó chyán?

什麼地方我能[以最好比滙率]換外國錢?

272. What is the exchange rate on the dollar?

í-kwài měi jīn kě hwàn dwō-shau?

一塊美金可換多少？

273. Can I cash [a personal check]?

wǒ kě bu ké-yi yùng [sž-rén jř-pyàu] hwàn syàn-kwǎn?

我可不可以用［私人支票］換現款？

274. —a traveler's check.

—lyǔ-syíng jř-pyàu. 一旅行支票.

275. I have [a bank draft].

wǒ yǒu [yì-jāng yín-háng běn-pyàu].

我有［一張銀行本票］.

276. —a letter of credit.

—syìn-yùng jwàng. 一信用狀.

277. I would like to exchange [twenty] dollars.

wǒ syǎng yàu hwàn [èr-shŕ-kwài] chyán.

我想要換［二十塊］錢.

278. Please give me [large bills].

chǐng gěi wǒ [dà myàn-é de chāu-pyàu].

請給我［大面額的鈔票］.

279. —small bills.

—syǎu myàn-é de chāu-pyàu. 一小面額的鈔票.

280. —small change.

—syǎu líng chyán. 小零錢.

281. —ten ywan.*

—shŕ ywán. 一十圓.

282. —twenty New Taiwan dollars.

èr-shŕ-kwài syīn tái bèi. 二十塊新台幣.

* See note, p. 37.

SHOPPING

1283. Show me [the hat] in the window.
chǐng bǎ dzài chwāng-lǐ de [màu-dz] gěi wǒ kàn-kàn.
請 把 在 窗 裏 的 [帽子] 給 我 看看.

1284. I am looking around.
wǒ jǐ shì kàn-kàn. 我 只 是 看看.

1285. I've been waiting a long time.
wǒ děng le háu jyǒu. 我 等 了 好 久.

1286. What brand do you have?
nǐ-men yǒu néi-jǔng pái-dz de? 你 們 有 那 種 牌子的?

1287. How much is it [per piece]?
dwō-shau chyán [měi yì-jǐ]? 多少 錢 [每 一 支] ?

1288. —per meter. —měi yì-gūng-chǐ. — 每 一 公尺.

1289. —per pound. —měi yí-bàng. — 每 一 磅.

1290. —per kilo. —měi yì-gūng-jīn. — 每 一 公斤.

1291. —per package. —měi yì-bāu. — 每 一 包.

1292. —per bunch. —měi yí-chwàr. — 每 一 串.

1293. —per jin.* —měi jīn. — 每 斤.

1294. —per chr.† —měi chǐ. — 每 尺.

1295. —per sheng.‡ —měi shēng. — 每 升.

1296. (It is) too expensive.
tài gwèi le! 太 貴 了 !

---

* *Jin* is a Chinese measure of weight equivalent to 0.5 kilo or 1.1 lbs.
† *Chǐ* is a Chinese measure of length a little over one foot.
‡ Cubic measure equal to 0.9 of a quart.

1297. It is cheap. pyán-yì. 便宜.

1298. It is reasonable.
jyà-chyán gūng-dàu. 價錢公道.

1299. Is that your lowest price?
nèi shr̀ dzwèi dī jyà-gé ma? 那是最低價格嗎?

1300. Do you allow a discount?
yǒu méi-yǒu dǎ jé-kou? 有沒有打折扣?

1301. I [do not] like that.
wǒ [bù-dà] syǐ-hwān nèi-ge. 我[不大]喜歡那個.

1302. Have you something [better] than this?
nín yǒu méi-yǒu bǐ jèi-ge [gèng hǎu]?
您有沒有比這個[更好]?

1303. —cheaper. —gèng pyán-yì. -更便宜.

1304. —more chic. —gèng syáu-sǎ. -更瀟洒.

1305. —softer. —gèng róu-rwǎn. -更柔軟.

1306. —stronger. —gèng jyān-gù. -更堅固.

1307. —heavier. —gèng jùng. -更重.

1308. —lighter (in weight).
—gèng chīng de. - 更輕的.

1309. —tighter. —gèng jǐn de. -更緊的.

1310. —looser. —gèng kwān-dà de. -更寬大的.

1311. —lighter (in color).
—gèng chyǎn sè de. - 更淺色的.

1312. —darker. —gèng shēn sè de. -更深色的.

1313. Do you have this [in my size]?
jèi-jyàn yǒu méi-yǒu [wǒ de chř-tswùn]?
這件有沒有[我的尺寸]?

1314. —in a larger size.

—chř-tswùn bí-jyău dà yì-dyăr de.

一尺寸比較大一點兒的.

1315. —in a smaller size.

—chř-tswùn bí-jyău syǎu yì-dyăr de.

一尺寸比較小一點兒的.

1316. —in another color.

—lìng-wài yì-jǔng yán-sè de. —另外一種顏色的.

1317. —in a different style.

—byé de shr̀-yàng. —別的式樣.

1318. Where is the fitting room?

shr̀ yī-fáng dzài năr? 試衣房在那兒?

1319. May I try it on?

wŏ kě shr̀ chwān yí-syà ma? 我可試穿一下嗎?

1320. It does not fit.

jèi-jyàn bu hé-shr̀. 這件不合適.

1321. Too [short] [long] [big] [small].

tài [dwăn] [cháng] [dà] [syǎu]. 太[短][長][大][小].

1322. Can I order the same thing [in size 42]?

wŏ ké-yi dìng yí-jyàn [sz̀-shŕ-èr chř-tswùn de] ma?

我可以定一件[四十二尺寸的]嗎?

1323. Please take my measurements.

chǐng tì wŏ lyáng shēn. 請替我量身.

1324. The length. cháng. 長.

1325. The width. kwān. 寬.

1326. The height. gāu. 高.

1327. The depth. shēn dù. 深度.

1328. Will it [shrink] [break]?

hwèi bu hwèi [swō-dwăn] [swèi]? 會不會[縮短][碎]?

1329. Are these handmade?
jèi-syē shr̀ bu-shr̀ shǒu jr̀ de? 這些是不是手製的？

1330. Is it [new]?
shr̀ bu-shr̀ [syīn de]? 是不是 [新 的]？

1331. —second hand.
—èr shǒu hwò. — 二手貨

1332. —an antique. —gú-dǔng. 一古董

1333. —a replica. —fù-jr̀ pǐn. 一複製品

1334. —an imitation.
—fǎng dzàu pǐn. 一仿造品

1335. Is this color-fast?
shr̀-fǒu bù twèi sè? 是否不褪色？

1336. This is [not] my size.
jèi [bu shr̀] wǒ de chǐ-tswùn. 這 [不是] 我的尺寸

1337. Please have this ready soon.
chǐng gǎn-kwài bǎ jèi-jyàn dzwò hǎu.
請趕快把這件做好

1338. How long will it take to make the alterations?
syōu-gǎi syū-yàu dwō jyǒu? 修改需要多久？

1339. Does the price include [alterations]?
jèi-ge jyà-chyán shr̀-fǒu bāu-kwò [syōu-gǎi]?
這個價錢是否包括 [修改]？

1340. I cannot decide.
wǒ bù néng jywé-dìng. 我不能決定

1341. I'll wait until it is ready.
wǒ děng dàu hǎu. 我等到好

1342. Wrap this.
chǐng bǎ jèi-ge bāu chǐ-lái. 請把這個包起來

1343. Where do I pay?
wǒ dàu nǎr chyù fù-chyán? 我到那兒去付錢？

1344. Do I pay [the salesman]?

wǒ shr̀ bu-shr̀ fù gěi [dyàn-ywán]?

我是不是付給[店員]?

1345. —the salesgirl.

—nyǔ-dyàn-ywán.- 女店員.

1346. —the cashier.   —chū-nà-ywán.- 出納員.

1347. Will you accept this credit card?

jyē bu jyē-shòu jèi-jāng syìn-yùng-kǎ?

接不接受這張信用卡?

1348. May I pay with a personal check?

wǒ shr̀-fǒu ké-yi yùng sz̄-rén jr̆-pyàu?

我是否可以用私人支票?

1349. Is this identification acceptable?

nín jyē-shòu bu jyē-shòu jèi-ge shēn-fèn-jèng?

您接受不接受這個身份証?

1350. Is the reference sufficient?

bǎu-jèng-rén gòu bu gòu? 保証人够不够?

1351. Can you send it to my hotel?

nín ké-yi bǎ jèi-jyàn sùng dàu wǒ de lyú-gwǎn ma?

您可以把這件送到我的旅館嗎?

1352. Can you ship it [to New York City]?

nín ké-yi bǎ jèi-jyàn yùn [dàu nyǒu-ywe shr̀] ma?

您可以把這件運[到紐約市]嗎?

1353. Pack this carefully for export.

syǎu-syīn de bǎ jèi-jyàn dǎ hǎu yǐ byàn shū-chū.

小心的把這件打好以便輸出.

1354. Give me [a bill] [a credit memo].

gěi wǒ [jàng-dān] [syìn-yùng jwàng].

給我[賬單][信用狀].

1355. I shall pay upon delivery.

sùng dá shŕ wǒ tsái fù-chyán. 送達時我才付錢.

1356. Is there an additional charge for delivery?
sùng dá yǒu méi-yǒu lìng-wài shōu fèi?
送達有沒有另外收費？

1357. I wish to return this article.
wǒ syǎng yàu twèi-hwéi jèi-jyàn wù pǐn.
我想要退回這件物品．

1358. Refund my money.
fù hwán wǒ de chyán. 付還我的錢．

1359. Please exchange this.
chǐng bǎ jèi-jyàn hwàn yí-syà. 請把這件換一下．

CLOTHING AND ACCESSORIES

1360. A bathing cap. syí-dzǎu màu. 洗澡帽．

1361. A bathing suit. yóu-yǔng yī. 游泳衣

1362. [An elastic] belt.
[sūng jǐn] dài. 鬆緊帶

1363. A blouse. dwǎn shān. 短衫．

1364. Boots. sywē-dz. 靴子．

1365. Bracelet. shǒu-lyàn. 手鍊

1366. A brassiere. nǎi-jàu. 奶罩

1367. Briefs. dwǎn-kù. 短褲．

1368. A button. nyǒu-kòu. 鈕扣

1369. A cane. shǒu-jàng. 手杖

1370. A cap. syǎu-màu. 小帽

1371. Children's clothes. túng-jwāng. 童裝．

1372. A coat. dà-yī. 大衣．

1373. A collar. yī-lǐng. 衣領.

1374. Cufflinks. syòu-kòu. 袖扣.

1375. A dress. yī-shang. 衣裳.

1376. Chinese long dress. chí-páu. 祺袍.

1377. Earrings. ěr-hwán. 耳環.

1378. A girdle. swō-fú. 縮腹.

1379. [A pair of] gloves.
[yì-shwāng] shǒu-tàu. [一双] 手套.

1380. A handkerchief. shǒu-jīn. 手巾.

1381. A jacket. gwà-dz. 褂子.

1382. A Chinese jacket. mǎ-gwà-dz. 馬褂子.

1383. A dinner jacket. nán-lǐ-fú. 男禮服.

1384. Jewelry. jū-bǎu lèi. 珠寶類.

1385. Lingerie. nyǔ-nèi-yī. 女内衣.

1386. A money clip. chyán-jyā-dz. 錢夾子.

1387. A necktie. lǐng-dài. 領帶.

1388. A nightgown. nyǔ-shwèi-yī. 女睡衣.

1389. Pajamas. shwèi-yī kù. 睡衣褲.

1390. Panties. nyǔ kù. 女褲.

1391. A pin (decorative).
hwā-byé-jēn. 花別針.

1392. A safety pin. byé-jēn. 別針.

1393. A straight pin. kòu-jēn. 扣針.

1394. A raincoat. yǔ-yī. 雨衣.

1395. Ribbon. dwàn-dài. 緞帶.

1396. A ring. jyè-jr. 戒指.

1397. Rubbers. jyău-syé. 膠鞋.

1398. Sandals. lyáng-syé. 涼鞋

1399. A scarf (OR: **shawl**). wéi-jīn. 圍巾

1400. A shirt. chèn-shān. 襯衫

1401. Shoelaces. syé-dài. 鞋帶

1402. Shoes. pí-syé. 皮鞋

1403. A skirt. chyún-dz. 裙子

1404. A slip. nyŭ-rén de chèn-chyún. 女人的襯裙

1405. Slippers. twō-syé. 拖鞋

1406. Socks. dwăn wā. 短襪

1407. Stockings. cháng wā. 長襪

1408. A man's suit. syī-jwāng. 西裝

1409. A sweater. máu-yī. 毛衣

1410. [A pair of] trousers.
yì-tyáu cháng kù. 一條長褲

1411. An umbrella. yì-bă săn-dz. 一把傘子

1412. An undershirt. hàn-shān. 汗衫

1413. Undershorts. dwăn nèi-kù. 短內褲

1414. Men's underwear. ˋnán-nèi-yī. 男內衣

1415. A wallet. chyán-bāu. 錢包.

COLORS

1416. Black. hēi sè. 黑色.

1417. [Light] [Dark] [Medium] blue.
[chyăn] [shēn] [jūng] lán sè. [淺] [深] [中] 藍色.

1418. Brown. dzūng sè. 棕色.

1419. Cream. nǎi-yóu sè. 奶油色.

1420. Gray. hwēi sè. 灰色.

1421. Green. lyù sè. 綠色.

1422. Olive. gán-lǎn sè. 橄欖色.

1423. Orange. syìng-hwáng. 杏黃.

1424. Pink. fěn-húng. 粉紅.

1425. Purple. dž sè. 紫色.

1426. Red. húng sè. 紅色.

1427. Tan. hwáng hé sè. 黃褐色.

1428. White. bái sè. 白色.

1429. Yellow. hwáng sè. 黃色.

MATERIALS

1430. Metal. jīn-shǔ. 金屬.

1431. Aluminum. lyǔ. 鋁.

1432. Brass. hwáng-túng. 黃銅.

1433. Copper. húng-túng. 紅銅.

1434. Gold. jīn-dz. 金子.

1435. Iron. tyě. 鐵.

1436. Silver. yín-dz. 銀子.

1437. Steel. gāng. 鋼.

1438. [Synthetic] textiles.
[rén-jàu de] fǎng-jř-pǐn. [人造的] 紡織品.

1439. Cotton. myán-bù. 棉布.

1440. Dacron. dá-kè-lúng. 達克龍.

1441. Nylon. ní-lúng. 尼龍.

1442. Orlon. àu-lúng. 奧龍.

1443. Silk. sz-jr-pǐn. 絲織品.

1444. Wool. yáng-máu. 羊毛.

1445. Ceramics (OR: **Pottery**).
táu chì. 陶器.

1446. China (OR: **Porcelain**).
tsź-chì. 瓷器.

1447. Crystal. shwěi-jīng. 水晶.

1448. Fur. máu. 毛.

1449. Glass. bwō-li. 玻璃.

1450. Leather. pí. 皮.

1451. Plastic. sù-jyāu. 塑膠.

1452. Stone. shŕ-tóu. 石頭.

1453. Wood. mù-tóu. 木頭.

BOOKSHOP, STATIONER, NEWSDEALER

1454. Do you have any [books] in English?
nǐ-men yǒu méi-yǒu yīng-wén [shū]?
你們有沒有英文 [書]？

1455. I am just browsing.
wǒ jǐ shr kàn-kàn. 我只是看看.

1456. Playing cards. jǐ-pái. 紙牌.

1457. A dictionary. yì-běn dž-dyǎn. 一本字典.

1458. [A dozen] envelopes.
[yì-dá] syìn-fēng. [一打] 信封.

1459. An eraser. syàng-pí. 橡皮.

1460. Fiction. jwàn chí syǎu-shwō. 傳奇小說.

1461. Folders. jywàn dzūng. 卷宗.

1462. A guidebook.
lyǔ-syíng jř-nán. 旅行指南.

1463. Ink. mwò-shwěi. 墨水.

1464. A map. dì-tú. 地圖.

1465. Some magazines. yì-syē dzá-jř. 一些雜誌.

1466. A newspaper. yí-fèn bàu-jř. 一份報紙.

1467. Nonfiction.
fēi jwàn chí syǎu-shwō. 非傳奇小說.

1468. A notebook.
yì-běn bǐ-jì-bù (OR: bǐ-jì běn-dz). 一本筆記簿 (筆記本子).

1469. Airmail stationery.
háng-kūng yóu jyàn wén-jyù. 航空郵件文具.

1470. [Note] [Carbon] [Onionskin] paper.
[bǐ-jì] [fù-syé] [tsūng pí] jř. [筆記][複寫][葱皮] 紙.

1471. [Writing] [Wrapping] paper.
[syě-dž yùng] [bāu jwāng] jř. [寫字用][包裝] 紙.

1472. A fountain pen.
yì-jř gāng-bǐ. 一枝鋼筆.

1473. A ballpoint pen.
yì-jř ywán-dž-bǐ. 一枝原子筆.

1474. A pencil. yì-jř chyān-bǐ. 一枝鉛筆.

1475. Scotch tape. jyāu dài. 膠帶.

1476. String. shéng-dz. 繩子.

1477. Thread. syàn. 線.

1478. Typewriter [ribbon].
dǎ-dz̀-jī [dài]. 打字机 [帶].

PHARMACY

1479. Is there [a pharmacy] here where they understand English?
jèr yǒu méi-yǒu [yàu-fáng] dǔng de yīng-wén?
這兒有沒有 [藥房] 懂 的 英文?

1480. I would like to speak to a [male] [female] clerk.
wǒ syǎng gēn yí-ge [nán] [nyǔ] dyàn-ywán jyǎng.
我想跟一個 [男] [女] 店員講.

1481. Can you fill this prescription [immediately]?
nín kě bu ké-yi [gǎn-kwài] jàu fāng bǎ yàu pèi hǎu?
您可不可以 [趕快] 照方把藥配好?

1482. Is it [mild] [safe]?
(yàu) [wēn-hwó] [ān-chyán] ma?
(藥) [溫和] [安全] 嗎?

1483. Antibiotic. kàng shēng sù. 抗生素.

1484. Sleeping pill. ān-mín yàu. 安眠藥.

1485. Tranquilizer. jèn-jìng jì. 鎮靜劑.

1486. Poison. dú-yàu. 毒藥.

1487. Take according to directions.
chǐng àn-jàu jǐ-shr̀. 請按照指示.

1488. Not to be taken internally.
bù kě nèi fù. 不可內服.

DRUGSTORE ITEMS

1489. Adhesive tape (OR: **Band-aid**).
jyāu bù. 膠布

1490. Alcohol. jyǒu-jīng. 酒精

1491. Antiseptic. syāu-dú jì. 消毒劑

1492. Aspirin. jǐ tùng yàu. 止痛藥

1493. Bandages. bēng-dài. 繃帶

1494. Bath oil. mù-yù yóu. 沐浴油

1495. Bath salts. mù-yù yán. 沐浴鹽

1496. Bicarbonate of soda.
tàn-swān-chīng-nà. 碳酸氫鈉

1497. Bobby pins (OR: **Hair clips**).
chyǎ-dz. 夾子

1498. Boric acid. péng swān. 硼酸

1499. Chewing gum. kǒu syāng. 口香

1500. Cleaning fluid.
chīng-jìng yì. 清淨液

1501. Cleansing tissues.
chīng-jìng shā jǐ. 清淨紗紙

1502. Cold cream.
lěng syāng (OR: sywě-hwā-gāu). 冷霜（雪花膏）

1503. Cologne. gē-lúng syāng shwěi. 哥龍香水

1504. Comb. shū-dz. 梳子

1505. Compact. fěn hé. 粉盒

1506. Contraceptives. yàu-wù jǐ.

1507. Corn pad. jī-yǎn bāu. 雞眼包

1508. Cotton (absorbent).
myán-hwā. 棉花

1509. Cough syrup. ké-sòu yàu. 咳嗽葯

1510. Deodorant. fáng chòu jì. 防臭劑

1511. Depilatory. twō máu yàu. 脫毛葯

1512. Disinfectant. syāu-dú yàu. 消毒葯

1513. Ear plugs. ěr sài. 耳塞

1514. Enema bag. gwàn cháng chì. 灌腸器

1515. Epsom salts. syè yán. 瀉鹽

1516. Eye cup. syǐ yǎn bēi. 洗眼杯

1517. Eye wash. syǐ yǎn yàu. 洗眼葯

1518. Gauze. shā bù. 紗布

1519. Hairbrush. fǎ shwā. 髮刷

1520. Hair tonic. shēng fǎ yàu. 生髮葯

1521. Hair net. fǎ wǎng. 髮網

1522. Hair pins. fǎ jēn. 髮釘

1523. Hair spray. fǎ jyāu-shwěi. 髮膠水

1524. Hand lotion. měi shǒu jì. 美手劑

1525. Hot-water bottle.
rè shwěi píng. 熱水瓶

1526. Ice bag. bīng dài. 冰袋

1527. Insecticide. shā chúng yàu. 殺蟲葯

1528. Iodine. dyàn jyǒu. 碘酒

1529. Laxative. syè yàu. 瀉葯

1530. Lipstick. chwún-gāu. 唇膏

1531. Medicine dropper.
dyǎn yàu píng. 點葯瓶

1532. Mouthwash. shù-kǒu jì. 漱口剂.

1533. Nail file. jǐ-jya tswò-dz. 指甲锉子.

1534. Nail polish. jǐ-jya yóu. 指甲油.

1535. Nose drops. dī bí yàu. 滴鼻药.

1536. Ointment (OR: **Cream**).
yàu-gāu. 药膏.

1537. Peroxide.
gwò yǎng hwà chīng. 过氧化氢.

1538. [Face] [Foot] [Talcum] powder.
[syāng] [jyǎu] [pū] fěn. [香] [脚] [扑] 粉.

1539. Powder puff. fěn pū. 粉扑.

1540. [Straight] [Electric] [Safety] razor.
[jí] [dyàn] [ān-chywán] tì dāu. [直] [电] [安全] 剃刀.

1541. Razor blade. tì dāu pyàn. 剃刀片.

1542. Rouge. yān-jr. 胭脂.

1543. Sanitary napkins.
wèi-shēng jīn. 衛生巾.

1544. Scissors. jyǎn-dāu. 剪刀.

1545. Sedative. jèn-jìng yàu. 镇静药.

1546. Shampoo. syǐ fǎ jì. 洗髮剂.

1547. Shaving brush.
syōu myàn shwā. 修面刷.

1548. Shaving [cream] [lotion].
tì hú [gāu] [jì]. 剃鬍 [膏] [剂].

1549. Shower cap. lìn-yù màu. 淋浴帽.

1550. Smelling salts. chòu yán. 嗅盐.

1551. Soap. féi-dzàu. 肥皂.

1552. Sponge. hǎi myán. 海綿.

1553. Sunburn ointment.
fáng shài gāu. 防晒膏.

1554. Sunglasses. tài-yáng yǎn-jìng. 太陽眼鏡.

1555. Syringe. jù-sè chì. 注射器.

1556. Thermometer. hán-shú-byǎu. 寒暑表.

1557. Toothbrush. yá-shwā. 牙刷.

1558. Toothpaste. yá-gāu. 牙膏.

1559. Toothpowder. yá-fěn. 牙粉.

1560. Vaseline. fán-shr̀-lín jŕ. 凡士林脂.

1561. Vitamins. wéi-tā-mìng. 維他命.

1562. Washcloth. máu-jīn. 毛巾.

CAMERA SHOP AND PHOTOGRAPHY

1563. I want a roll of film [for this camera].
wǒ yàu yí-jywàn jyāu-jywǎn fàng [dzài jèi-ge jàu-syàng-jī lí].
我要一卷膠捲放[在這個照相机裏]

1564. Do you have [color film]?
nǐ-men yǒu méi-yǒu [tsǎi sè rwǎn-pyàn]?
你們有没有[彩色軟片]?

1565. —black-and-white film.
—hēi bái rwǎn-pyàn. 一黑白軟片.

1566. —movie film.
—dyàn-yǐng jyāu-pyàn. 一電影膠片.

1567. What is the charge [for developing a roll]?
[syǐ yí-jywàn] syū-yàu dwō-shǎu chyán?
[洗一卷] 需要多少錢？

1568. —for enlarging. —fàng dà. —放大．

1569. —for one print.
—shài yì-jāng syàng-pyàn. —晒一張相片．

1570. May I take a photo of you?
wǒ syǎng tì nín pāi-yi-pāi, hǎu bu hǎu?
我想替您拍一拍，好不好？

1571. Would you take a photo of me, please?
chǐng nín tì wǒ pāi yì-jāng, hǎu bu hǎu?
請您替我拍一張，好不好？

1572. A color print.
yì-jāng tsǎi sè syàng-pyàn. 一張彩色相片．

1573. Flashbulbs. shǎn gwāng dēng. 閃光燈．

1574. The lens. jìng-tóu. 鏡頭．

1575. The negative. dǐ-pyàn. 底片．

1576. The shutter. gwāng-chywān. 光圈．

1577. A transparency.
tòu-míng wù tǐ. 透明物体．

1578. A tripod. sān-jyǎu jyà. 三腳架．

GIFT AND SOUVENIR LIST

1579. Basket. lán-dz. 籃子．

1580. Box of candy.
yì-hé táng-gwǒ. 一盒糖果．

1581. Doll. yáng wá-wá. 洋娃娃.

1582. Embroidery. syòu-hwā. 綉花.

1583. Handicrafts. shǒu-gūng pǐn. 手工品.

1584. Needlework. jēn-syàn-hwó. 針線火.

1585. Penknife. syāu chyān-bǐ dāu. 削鉛筆刀.

1586. Perfume. syāng shwěi. 香水.

1587. Phonograph records.
chàng-pyàn. 唱片.

1588. Precious stone. bǎu shŕ. 宝石.

1589. Print (graphics). tú-àn. 圖案.

1590. Reproduction (of painting, etc.).
fān yìn. 翻印.

1591. Souvenir. jì-nyàn pǐn. 紀念品.

1592. Toys. wán-jyù. 玩具.

CIGAR STORE

1593. Where is the nearest cigar store?
dzwèi jìn de syāng yān dyàn dzài nǎr?
最近的香煙店在那兒?

1594. I want some cigars.
wǒ yàu yì-syē syāng yān. 我要一些香煙.

1595. What brands of American cigarettes [with menthol] do you have?
nǐ-men yǒu nèi-jǔng pái de měi-gwo [bwó-hé] yān?
你們有那種牌的美囯[薄荷]煙?

1596. One pack of king-size [filter-tip] cigarettes.
yì-bāu [yǒu lyù dzwěi de] cháng syāng yān.
一包［有濾嘴的］長香煙。

1597. I need a lighter.
wǒ syū-yàu yí-ge dyán-hwǒ jī. 我需要一個點火机。

1598. Lighter fluid.   dá-hwǒ jī yóu. 打火机油。

1599. Flint.   hwǒ shŕ. 火石。

1600. A pipe.   yān-dǒu. 煙斗。

1601. Pipe cleaners.
chīng yān-dǒu de dūng-syi. 清煙斗的東西。

1602. Pipe tobacco.   yān tsǎu. 煙草。

1603. A tobacco pouch.   yān tsǎu dài. 煙草袋。

LAUNDRY AND DRY CLEANING

**1604. Where can I take my laundry to be cleaned
(LIT.: Where is the laundry)?**
syǐ-yī dyàn dzài nǎr? 洗衣店在那兒？

1605. Is there a dry-cleaning service near here?
dzài jèr fù-jìn yǒu méi-yǒu gān-syǐ dyàn?
在這兒附近有没有乾洗店？

**1606. Wash this blouse in [hot] [warm] [lukewarm]
[cold] water.**
chǐng yùng [rè] [nwǎn] [wēn] [lěng] shwěi syǐ jèi-jyàn nyǔ-
chèn-shān.
請用［熱］［暖］［溫］［冷］水洗這件女襯衫。

1607. No starch, please.
chǐng bú yàu jyāng. 請不要漿。

1608. Remove this stain [from this shirt].

chǐng bǎ [jèi-jyàn chèn-shān de] dzāng-r chyù.

請把 [這件襯衫的] 髒去

1609. Press [the trousers].

chǐng bǎ [jèi-tyáu kù-dz] tàng píng.

請把 [這條褲子] 燙平

1610. Starch [my collar].

chǐng bǎ [lǐng-dz] jyāng-yìng. 請把 [領子] 漿硬

1611. Dry clean [this coat].

chǐng bǎ [jèi-jyàn dà-yī] gān-syǐ. 請把 [這件大衣] 乾洗

1612. [The belt] is missing.

[yāu-dài] bú jyàn le! [腰帶] 不見了!

1613. Sew on [this button].

chǐng bǎ [jèi-ge nyǒu-kòu] féng shàng.

請把 [這個鈕扣] 縫上

REPAIRS AND ADJUSTMENTS

1614. This does not work (LIT.: **This is broken**).

jèi-ge hwài le! 這個壞了!

1615. This watch [is fast] [is slow].

jèi-ge shóu-byǎu [tài kwài] [tài màn].

這個手錶 [太快] [太慢]

1616. [My glasses] are broken.

[wǒ de yǎn-jìng-r] pwò le. [我的眼鏡兒] 破了

1617. It is torn. sz-pwò le. 撕破了

1618. Where can I get it repaired?

dzài nǎr ké-yǐ syōu-lǐ? 在那兒可以修理?

1619. Please fix [this lock].

chǐng bǎ [jèi-ge swǒ] syōu hǎu. 請把 [這個鎖] 修好

1620. Fix [the sole].
chǐng bǎ [jèi-ge syé-dǐ] syōu-lǐ. 請把[這個鞋底]修理.

1621. —the heel. —jèi-ge hòu-gēn. 這個後跟.

1622. —the uppers.
—syé-dz de shàng bù. 鞋子的上部.

1623. —the strap. —pí dài. 皮帶.

1624. Adjust [this hearing aid].
tyáu-jěng [jèi-ge jù tīng chì]. 調整[這個助聽器].

1625. Lengthen [this skirt].
chǐng bǎ [jèi-jyàn chyún-dz] gǎi cháng.
請把[這件裙子]改長.

1626. Shorten [the sleeves].
chǐng bǎ [jèi syòu-dz] gǎi dwǎn. 請把[這袖子]改短.

1627. Replace [the lining].
chǐng bǎ [lǐ-dz] gèng hwàn. 請把[裏子]更換.

1628. Mend [the pocket].
chǐng bǎ [yī-dài] syōu bǔ. 請把[衣袋]修補.

1629. Fasten it together.
chǐng jyé dzài yì-chí. 請結在一起.

1630. Clean [the mechanism].
chǐng bǎ [jèi-ge jī-chì] lùng chīng-jyé.
請把[這個机器]弄清潔.

1631. Lubricate [the spring].
chǐng dzài [jèi tán-hwáng] tú shàng hwá-yóu.
請在[這彈簧]塗上滑油.

1632. An alteration (clothing).
gēng gǎi yī-sháng. 更改衣裳.

1633. Needle. jēn. 針.

1634. Thimble. jēn gū. 針箍.

BARBER SHOP

1635. A haircut, please.
wǒ yàu lǐ-fà. 我要理髮

1636. A light trim.
syōu jyǎn yí-syà. 修剪一下.

1637. A shave. gwā hú-dz. 刮鬍子

1638. A shoeshine. tsā syé-dz. 擦鞋子

1639. Don't cut much [off the top] [on the sides].
[shàng bù de] [páng-byār de] bú-yàu jyǎn tài dwō.
[上部的] [旁边的] 不要剪太多.

1640. I want to keep my hair long.
wǒ syǎng yàu bǎ tóu-fà lyóu cháng.
我想要把頭髮留長.

1641. I part my hair [on this side].
wǒ de tóu-fà [dzài jè-lǐ] fēn byān.
我的頭髮 [在這裏] 分邊.

1642. —on the other side.
—dzài nèi-byār. - 在那边兒

1643. —in the middle.
—dzài jūng-jyān. - 在中間.

1644. No hair tonic. méi-yǒu fà yóu. 没有髮油.

1645. Trim [my mustache (OR: beard)].
syōu jyǎn [wǒ de hú-dz]. 修剪 [我的鬍子].

1646. —my eyebrows.
—wǒ de méi-mau. - 我的眉毛.

1647. —my sideburns.
—wǒ de lyǎng bìng. - 我的兩鬢

1648. Scissors only, please.
chǐng jǐ yùng jyǎn-dāu. 請只用剪刀.

BEAUTY PARLOR

1649. Can I make an appointment for [Monday] afternoon?

wǒ syǎng hé nín dìng yí-ge ywē-hwèi dzài [syīng-chī-yī] syà-wǔ.

我想和您定一個約會在[星期一]下午.

1650. [Comb] [Wash] my hair.

chǐng [shū] [syǐ] wǒ de tóu-fà. 請[梳][洗]我的頭髮

1651. Shampoo and set, please.

chǐng syǐ tsā tóu bù gēn tàng tóu-fà.

請洗擦頭部跟燙頭髮

1652. Not too short.

bú-yàu tài dwǎn. 不要太短.

1653. In this style, please.

chǐng dzwò jèi-ge shr̀-yàng. 請做這個式樣.

1654. Dye my hair [in this shade].

chǐng bǎ wǒ de tóu-fà rǎn [chéng jèi-ge yán-sè].

請把我的頭髮染[成這個顏色].

1655. Clean and set this wig.

chǐng bǎ jèi-ge jyǎ fà lùng chīng-jyé gēn shǐ chéng bwō làng syíng.

請把這個假髮弄清潔跟使成波浪形.

1656. A curl. jywǎn fà. 鬈髮.

1657. A facial. lyǎn bù ān-mwó. 臉部按摩

1658. A hairpiece. jyǎ fà. 假髮.

1659. Hair rinse. pyàu chīng tóu-fà. 漂清頭髮

1660. A manicure. syōu jǐ-jya. 修指甲

1661. A massage. ān-mwó. 按摩.

1662. A permanent wave.
dyàn tàng fà. 電燙髮.

STORES AND SERVICES

1663. Antique shop.
ṣú-dǔng dyàn pù. 古董店鋪.

1664. Art gallery. měi-shù-gwǎn. 美術館.

1665. Artist's materials.
měi-shù jyā yùng-jyù. 美術家用具.

1666. Auto rental. chū-dzū chì-chē. 出租汽車.

1667. Auto repairs. syōu-lǐ chì-chē. 修理汽車.

1668. Bakery.
myàn-bāu dyàn-syīn dyàn. 麵包點心店.

1669. Bank. yín-háng. 銀行.

1670. Bar. jyǒu-bā. 酒巴.

1671. Beauty salon.
měi-rúng ywàn. 美容院.

1672. Bookshop. shū dyàn. 書店.

1673. Butcher shop (for pork).
ṣū-ròu-pù. 豬肉鋪.

1674. Butcher shop (for beef and lamb).
yáng-ròu-pù. 羊肉鋪.

1675. Candy shop. táng-gwǒ dyàn. 糖果店.

1676. Checkroom.
yī màu jì fàng chù. 衣帽寄放處.

1677. Clothing store. bù dyàn. 布店.

1678. Children's clothing store.
syǎu-hái-dz bù dyàn. 小孩子布店.

1679. Men's clothing store.
nán-jwāng dyàn. 男裝店.

1680. Ladies' clothing store.
nyǚ-jwāng dyàn. 女裝店.

1681. Cosmetics. hwà-jwāng pǐn. 化粧品.

1682. Dance studio. wǔ shr̀. 舞室.

1683. Delicatessen.
syǎu shŕ-pǐn dyàn. 小食品店.

1684. Department store.
bǎi-hwò gūng-sž. 百貨公司.

1685. Dry cleaners. gān-syǐ dyàn. 乾洗店.

1686. Electrical supplies.
dyàn-chì yùng pǐn. 電器用品.

1687. Employment agency.
jŕ-yè jyè-shàu swǒ. 職業介紹所.

1688. Fish store. yú dyàn. 魚店.

1689. Florist. hwā dyàn. 花店.

1690. Fruit store. shwéi-gwǒ dyàn. 水果店.

1691. Funeral parlor. bìn-yí-gwǎn. 殯儀館.

1692. Furniture store. jyā-jyù dyàn. 家具店.

1693. Gift store. lǐ-wù dyàn. 礼物店.

1694. Grocery.
shŕ-pǐn dzá-hwò dyàn. 食品雜貨店.

1695. Ladies' hairdresser.
nyú-lǐ-fà shr̄. 女理髮師.

1696. Men's hairdresser.
nán-lǐ-fà shī. 男理髮師.

1697. Hardware store. wǔ-jīn dyàn. 五金店.

1698. Hat shop. màu dyàn. 帽店.

1699. Housewares.
yā-tíng yùng-jyù dyàn. 家庭用具店.

1700. Jewelry store. jū-bǎu dyàn. 珠寶店.

1701. Lawyer. lyù-shī. 律師.

1702. Laundry. syǐ-yī dyàn. 洗衣店.

1703. Loans. dài jīn. 貸金.

1704. Lumberyard. mù-tsái háng. 木材行.

1705. Market. shr-chǎng. 市場.

1706. Money exchange.
wàn chyán chù. 換錢處.

1707. Music store. yīn-ywè dyàn. 音樂店.

1708. Musical instruments. ywè chì. 樂器.

1709. Newsstand. mài bàu tān. 賣報攤.

1710. Oculist. yǎn kē yī-shēng. 眼科醫生.

1711. Paints. yóu-chī. 油漆.

1712. Pastry shop. gāu bǐng dyàn. 糕餅店.

1713. Pet shop. nyǎu shòu dyàn. 鳥獸店.

1714. Photographer. jàu-syàng shī. 照相師.

1715. Printing. yìn-shwā. 印刷.

1716. Real estate office.
dì-chǎn gūng-shī. 地產公司.

1717. Sewing machines. féng-yī jī. 縫衣机

1718. Shoemaker. syé-jyàng. 鞋匠

1719. Shoeshine. tsā syé. 擦鞋

1720. Shoe store. syé dyàn. 鞋店

1721. Shopping center.
lyán-hé shr̀-chǎng. 联合市場

1722. Sightseeing. yóu-lǎn. 遊覽

1723. Sign painter.
syě jāu-pái de rén. 寫招牌的人

1724. Sporting goods.
yùn-dùng yùng-jyù. 運動用具

1725. Stockbroker.
gǔ-pyàu jīng jì rén. 股票經紀人

1726. Supermarket.
chāu jí shr̀-chǎng. 超級市場

1727. Tailor (OR: **Dressmaker's**) **shop.**
tsái-feng pù. 裁縫舖

1728. Toy shop. wán-jyù dyàn. 玩具店

1729. Trucking. hwò yùn. 貨運

1730. Upholsterer.
shr̀ nèi jwāng-shr̀ shāng. 室内裝飾商

1731. Used cars. jyòu chē. 舊車

1732. Vegetable store. tsài dyàn. 菜店

1733. Watchmaker.
jūng byǎu jyàng. 鐘錶匠

1734. Liquor store. jyǒu dyàn. 酒店

BABY CARE

1735. I need a reliable babysitter tonight [at 7 o'clock].

wǒ jīn-tyān wǎn-shàng [chī-dyǎn] syū-yàu yí-ge kàu de jù jyàu gù yīng-hái de rén. 我今天晚上[七點]需要一個靠得住照顧嬰孩的人.

1736. Is diaper service available?

yǒu wú-nyàu-bù gùng yìng? 有無尿布供應?

1737. Call a pediatrician immediately.

chǐng gǎn-kwài jyàu yí-ge ér-kē yī-shŕ.
請趕快叫一個兒科醫生.

1738. Mix the formula.

tyáu jì chú fāng. 調擠處方.

1739. Sterilize the bottles and nipples.

chǐng bǎ nǎi-píng hé syàng-pí nǎi-tóu syāu-dú.
請把奶瓶和橡皮奶頭消毒.

1740. Change the diaper.

chǐng hwàn nyàu-bù. 請換尿布

1741. Bathe the baby.

chǐng tì yīng-ér syí-dzǎu. 請替嬰兒洗澡

1742. Put the baby in the crib for a nap (LIT.: **to sleep**).

chǐng bǎ yīng-ér fàng dzài yīng-chwáng shwèi-jyàu.
請把嬰兒放在嬰牀睡覺

1743. Give the baby a pacifier when he cries.

dāng yīng-ér kū shŕ, chǐng gěi tā yí-ge nǎi-tóu.
當嬰兒哭時,請給他一個奶頭.

1744. Do you have an ointment for diaper rash?

nín yǒu méi-yǒu yī-jŕ nyàu-bù fā jěn de yóu-gāu?
您有沒有醫治尿布發疹的油膏?

1745. Take the baby to the park in the carriage (OR: **stroller**).

chǐng yùng yīng-hái chē dài tā dàu gūng-ywán chyù.

请用婴孩車帶他到公園去.

1746. Baby (OR: **Strained**) **food.**

yù yīng shŕ pǐn. 育婴食品.

1747. Baby powder.

shwǎng-shēn fěn. 爽身粉.

1748. Bib. syūng wéi. 胸圍.

1749. Colic. wèi-chì. 胃痛.

1750. Disposable [bottles].

yùng hòu jí dyōu-dyàu de [píng-dz].

用後即丟揮的 [瓶子].

1751. High chair. yīng-ér dzwò yǐ. 婴兒座椅

1752. Nursemaid. kàn-mā. 看媽

1753. Playground. yóu-syì chǎng. 遊戲場

1754. Rattle. yǎu-gú. 搖鼓.

1755. Baby carrier (sling for carrying a child on one's back).

gwà yīng-hái de bèi dài. 掛婴孩的背帶.

1756. Stuffed toy.

tyán mǎn de wán-jyù. 填滿的玩具.

1757. Teething ring. chū yá chywān. 出牙圈.

HEALTH AND ILLNESS

1758. Is the doctor at [home] [his office]?

yī-shēng dzài bu dzài [jyā] [tā de yī-shř]?

医生在不在 [家] [他的医室] ?

1759. What are his office hours?

tā de mén-jěn shŕ-jyān shŕ shém-ma shŕ-hòu?

他的門診時間是什麼時候?

1760. I need a thermometer.

wǒ syū-yàu yí-ge hán-shú-byǎu. 我需要一個寒暑表.

1761. Take my temperature.

chǐng lyáng-lyáng wǒ de tǐ-wēn. 請量量我的體溫.

1762. I have something [in my eye].

yǒu dūng-syi [dzài wǒ de yǎn-jīng lǐ].

有東西[在我的眼睛裏].

1763. I have a pain [in my back] (LIT.: **My back hurts**).

[wǒ de bèi] swān tùng. [我的背]酸痛.

1764. [My toe] is swollen.

[wǒ de jyǎu-jř-tóu] jǔng le. [我的腳趾頭]腫了.

1765. It is sensitive to pressure.

dwèi yā-lì yǒu mín-gǎn. 對壓力有敏感.

1766. Is it serious?

shŕ bu-shŕ hěn yán-jùng? 是不是很嚴重?

1767. I do not sleep well.

wǒ shwèi bù hǎu. 我睡不好.

1768. I have no appetite.

wǒ méi-yǒu wèi-kǒu. 我沒有胃口.

1769. Can you give me some medication to relieve the pain?

nín shŕ-fǒu ké-yi gěi wǒ yì-syē yàu lái jř tùng?

您是否可以給我一些藥來止痛?

1770. Where should I have this prescription filled?

wǒ dàu nǎr mǎi jèi-syē yàu? 我到那兒買這些藥?

1771. Do I have to go to [a hospital]?

wǒ syū-yàu dàu [yī-ywàn] chyù ma?

我需要到[醫院]去嗎?

1772. Is it necessary to operate?

syū-yàu kāi-dāu ma? 需要開刀嗎？

1773. Must I stay in bed?

wǒ bì-syū tǎng dzài chwáng shàng ma?

我必須躺在牀上嗎？

1774. When will I begin to feel [better]?

wǒ shém-ma shŕ-hòu hwèi jywé de [hǎu yì-dyǎr]?

我什麼時候會覺得[好一點兒]？

1775. Is it contagious?

shŕ bu shŕ chwán-rǎn syìng de? 是不是傳染性的？

1776. I feel [worse] [about the same].

wǒ jywé de [gèng hwài] [chà-bu-dwō yí-yàng].

我覺得[更壞][差不多一樣].

1777. Shall I keep it bandaged?

wǒ syū-yàu bǎ jèi-ge yùng bēng-dài fú shàng ma?

我需要把這個用繃帶縛上嗎？

1778. Can I travel [on Monday]?

[syīng-chī-yī] wǒ ké-yi chyù lyǔ-syíng ma?

[星期一]我可以去旅行嗎？

1779. When will you come to see me again?

nín něi tyān dzài lái kàn wǒ? 您那天再來看我．

1780. When should I take [the medicine]?

wǒ shém-ma shŕ-hòu chŕ [yàu]? 我什麼時候吃[藥]

1781. —the pills. —wán yàu. 一丸藥

1782. Do I need [an injection]?

wǒ syū-yàu shŕ-syíng [jù-shè] ma? 我需要實行[注射]嗎

1783. Every hour.

měi yí-ge jūng-tóu. 每一個鐘頭．

1784. [Before] [After] meals (LIT.: **eating**).

chŕ-fàn [yǐ-chyán] [yǐ-hòu]. 吃飯[以前][以後].

1785. (At) bedtime.
shwèi-jyàu de shŕ-hòu. 睡覺的時候.

1786. On getting up.
chǐ chwáng de shŕ-hòu. 起床的時候.

1787. Twice a day.
yì-tyān lyǎng tsž. 一天兩次.

1788. An anesthetic. má-dzwèi yàu. 麻醉藥.

1789. Convalescence. hwěi-fu chī. 恢復期.

1790. Cure. jř-yù. 治癒.

1791. Diet. jyě shŕ. 節食.

1792. A drop. yì-dī. 一滴.

1793. A nurse. hù-shr. 護士.

1794. An orthopedist.
jěng syíng yī-shř. 整形医師.

1795. Remedy (OR: Treatment).
jř-lyáu. 治療.

1796. A specialist. jwān-jyā. 專家.

1797. A surgeon. wài-kē yī-shēng. 外科医生.

1798. A teaspoonful. yì-chá-chŕ. 一茶匙.

1799. X-ray. eks gwāng-syàn jyǎn-chá. X光綫檢查.

1800. Acupuncture. jēn-jyǒu. 針灸.

AILMENTS

1801. An abscess. núng jǔng. 膿腫.

1802. An allergy. gwò mǐn jèng. 過敏症.

1803. An appendicitis attack.
máng-cháng yán. 盲腸炎

1804. An insect bite. chúng yǎu. 蟲咬

1805. A blister. shwěi-pàu. 水泡

1806. A boil. yáng jǔng. 瘍腫

1807. A bruise. yū shāng. 瘀傷

1808. A burn. tàng shāng. 燙傷

1809. Chicken pox. shwěi-dòu. 水痘

1810. A chill. fā lěng. 發冷

1811. A cold. shāng-fēng. 傷風

1812. Constipation. byàn-jyé. 便結

1813. A corn. jī-yǎn. 雞眼

1814. A cough. ké-sòu. 咳嗽

1815. A cramp. chōu-jīn. 抽筋

1816. A cut. shāng-kǒu. 傷口

1817. Diarrhoea. bāi-lì. 白痢

1818. Dysentery. lì-jí. 痢疾

1819. An earache. ěr tùng. 耳痛

1820. An epidemic. chwān-rǎn-bìng. 傳染病

1821. To feel faint. yǎn-jīng hwā. 眼睛花

1822. A fever. fā-shāu. 發燒

1823. A fracture. tswò-shāng. 挫傷

1824. Hay fever. hwā-fěn rè. 花粉熱

1825. Headache. tóu tùng. 頭痛.

1826. Indigestion.
syāu-hwà bù lyǎng. 消化不良.

1827. Infection. chwán-rǎn. 傳染.

1828. Inflammation. húng jǔng. 紅腫.

1829. Influenza. gǎn-màu. 感冒.

1830. Insomnia. shř-mín jèng. 失眠症.

1831. Measles. má-jěn. 麻疹.

1832. German measles.
dé-gwo fēng-jěn. 德國風疹.

1833. Mumps. ěr syà syàn yán. 耳下腺炎.

1834. Nausea. dzwò ǒu. 作嘔.

1835. Nosebleed. bí sywě. 鼻血.

1836. Pneumonia. fèi-yán. 肺炎.

1837. Poisoning. jùng-dú. 中毒.

1838. A sprain. nyǒu-shāng. 扭傷.

1839. A sore throat.
hóu-tóu fá-yán. 喉頭發炎.

1840. A bee sting. fēng tsż. 蜂刺.

1841. A sunburn. shài-shāng. 晒傷.

1842. A swelling. jǔng. 腫.

1843. Tonsillitis.
byǎn-táu-syàn yán. 扁桃腺炎.

1844. Toothache. yá tùng. 牙痛.

1845. To vomit. ǒu. 嘔.

DENTIST

1846. Can you recommend [a good dentist]?

nín ké-yi jyè-shàu [yí-ge hǎu de yá-yī] ma? 您可以介紹 [一個好的牙医] 嗎?

1847. My [filling] has fallen out.

wǒ [tyán de yá] dyàu le. 我 [填的牙] 掉了.

1848. Can you replace the filling?

chǐng dzài bǎ tā tyán hǎu. 請再把它填好.

1849. Can you fix [the bridge]?

nín shr̀-fǒu ké-yi bǎ [chǐ-chyáu] syōu-lǐ? 您是否可以把 [齒橋] 修理?

1850. —this denture.

—jèi-yí-fù yǎ-yá. 一這一副假牙.

1851. This [tooth] hurts me.

jèi-ge [yá-chǐ] hěn tùng. 這個 [牙齒] 很痛.

1852. My gums are sore.

wǒ de yá-ròu hěn tùng. 我的牙肉很痛.

1853. I have [a broken tooth].

wǒ yǒu [yí-ge chǐ dwàn le]. 我有 [一個齒斷了].

1854. —a cavity.   —jèi-ge jù-chǐ. 一這個蛀齒.

1855. Please give me a [general] [local] anesthetic.

chǐng gěi wǒ [chywán shēn] [jyù bù] má-dzwèi. 請給我 [全身] [局部] 麻醉.

1856. I [do not] want the tooth extracted.

chǐng nín [bú] yàu bǎ jèi-ge yá-chǐ bá chū-lái. 請您 [不] 要把這個牙齒拔出來.

1857. A temporary filling. jàn-shŕ tyán hǎu jù-dùng. 暫時填好蛀洞

ACCIDENTS

1858. There has been an accident.
chū-shr̀ le! 出事了!

1859. Get [a doctor] immediately.
chǐng gǎn-kwài jyàu [yí-ge yī-shēng].
請趕快叫[一個醫生].

1860. —an ambulance.
—yí-ge jyòu-hù-chē. 一個救護車

1861. He has fallen. tā dyē-dǎu le. 他跌倒了.

1862. She has fainted. tā hwūn le. 她昏了.

1863. Do not move [her] [him].
bú yàu yú-dùng [tā] [tā].* 不要移動[她][他].

1864. [My finger] is bleeding.
[wǒ de shǒu-jř-tóu] chū sywě. [我的手指頭]出血

1865. A fracture [of the arm].
[bí-gù] tswò-shāng le. [臂骨]挫傷了.

1866. I want [to rest] [to sit down] [to lie down].
wǒ syǎng yàu [syōu-syi] [dzwò-syà] [tǎng-syà].
我想要[休息][坐下][躺下].

1867. Notify [my husband].
chǐng tūng-jr̄ [wǒ de syān-shēng].
請通知[我的先生].

1868. A tourniquet. jř-sywě dài. 止血帶.

* "He" (or "him") and "she" (or "her") are both pronounced *tā*, but the characters are different.

PARTS OF THE BODY

1869. Ankle. jyău-wàn. 脚.

1870. Appendix. máng-cháng. 盲腸.

1871. Arm. shóu-bǎng. 手膀.

1872. Armpit. gē-chř-wō. 胳肢窩.

1873. Artery. dùng-mài. 動脈.

1874. Back. bèi. 背.

1875. Belly. dǔ-dz. 肚子.

1876. Blood. sywě. 血.

1877. Blood vessel. sywé-gwǎn. 血管.

1878. Body. shēn-tǐ. 身体.

1879. Bone. gǔ-tou. 骨頭.

1880. Bowel. cháng-dz. 腸子.

1881. Breast. rǔ-fáng. 乳房.

1882. Buttocks. pì-gu. 屁股.

1883. Calf. syáu-twěi. 小腿.

1884. Cheek. sāi-jyá. 腮頰.

1885. Chest. syūng. 胸.

1886. Chin. syà-bā-gù kē-er. 下巴骨.

1887. Collarbone. swǒ-gù. 鎖骨.

1888. Ear. ěr. 耳.

1889. Elbow. jǒu. 肘.

1890. Eye. yǎn. 眼.

1891. Eyelashes. yǎn-máu. 眼毛.

1892. Eyelid. yǎn-pí. 眼皮.

1893. Face. lyǎn. 臉.

1894. Fingernail. jǐ-jya. 指甲.

1895. Foot. jyǎu. 脚.

1896. Forehead. nǎu-mén-dz. 腦門子.

1897. Gall bladder. dǎn-náng. 膽囊.

1898. Genitals. shēng-jí chì. 生殖器.

1899. Glands. syàn. 腺.

1900. Head. tóu. 頭.

1901. Heart. syīn. 心.

1902. Heel. jyǎu-hòu-gēn. 脚後跟.

1903. Hip. twún bù. 臀部.

1904. Intestines. cháng-dz. 腸子.

1905. Jaw. sāi-jyá. 腮頰.

1906. Joint. gū jyé. 骨節.

1907. Kidney. nèi-shèn. 內腎.

1908. Knee. syī. 膝.

1909. Larynx. hóu. 喉.

1910. Leg. twěi. 腿.

1911. Lip. dzwěi chwún. 嘴唇.

1912. Lungs. fèi. 肺.

1913. Mouth. kǒu. 口.

1914. Muscle. jī-ròu. 肌肉.

1915. Navel. dǔ-chí yǎn. 肚臍眼.

1916. Neck. bwó-dz. 脖子.

1917. Nerve. shén-jīng. 神經.

1918. Nose. bí-dz. 鼻子.

1919. Pancreas. yí. 胰

1920. Rib. lè-gǔ. 肋骨

1921. Shoulder. jyān-bǎng. 肩膀.

1922. Side. byār. 邊兒.

1923. Skin. pí-fū. 皮膚.

1924. Skull. nǎu-ké. 腦殼

1925. Spine. jí-gǔ. 脊骨.

1926. Spleen. pí. 脾

1927. Stomach. wèi. 胃

1928. Toe. jyǎu-jǐ-tou. 腳指頭

1929. Thigh. dà twěi. 大腿

1930. Throat. hóu-lung. 喉嚨

1931. Thumb. dà-mú-jǐ. 大栂指

1932. Tongue. shé-tóu. 舌頭

1933. Tonsils. byǎn-táu-syàn. 扁桃腺

1934. Vein. jìng-mài. 靜脈

1935. Waist. yāu. 腰

1936. Wrist. shǒu-wàn-dz. 手腕子

TIME

1937. What time is it?
shém-ma shŕ-hòu le? 什麼時候了?

1938. Two A.M.
dzǎu-shàng lyáng-dyǎn. 早上兩點.

1939. Two P.M.
syà-wǔ lyáng-dyǎn. 下午兩點.

1940. It is exactly half-past three.
jèng hǎu sān-dyǎn bàn. 正好三點半.

1941. Quarter-past four (LIT.: **Four fifteen**).
sz̀-dyǎn yí-kè (OR: sz̀-dyǎn shŕ-wǔ-fēn).
四點一刻 (四點十五分).

1942. Quarter to five (LIT.: **Four forty-five**).
sz̀-dyǎn sz̀-shŕ-wǔ-fēn. 四點四十五分.

1943. (At) ten (minutes) to six.
chà shŕ-fēn bú-dàu lyòu-dyǎn. 差十分不到六點.

1944. (At) twenty (minutes) past seven.
chī-dyǎn èr-shŕ-fēn. 七點二十分.

1945. It is early. hái dzǎu ne. 還早呢.

1946. It is late. tài wǎn le. 太晚了.

1947. In the morning. dzǎu-shàng. 早上.

1948. This afternoon.
jīn-tyān syà-wǔ. 今天下午

1949. Tomorrow. míng-tyān. 明天.

1950. Evening. wǎn-shàng. 晚上.

1951. (At) noon. jūng-wǔ. 中午.

1952. Midnight. bàn-yè. 半夜.

1953. During the day. bái-tyān. 白天.

1954. Every night.
měi-tyān wǎn-shàng. 每天晚上.

1955. All night. jěng yè. 整夜.

1956. Since yesterday.
tsúng dzwó-tyān kāi-shǐ. 從昨天開始.

1957. Last month. shàng-ge ywè. 上個月.

1958. Last year. chyù-nyán. 去年.

1959. Next Sunday. syà-ge syīng-chī-r̀. 下個星期日.

1960. Next week. syà-ge syīng-chī. 下個星期.

1961. The day before yesterday.
chyán-tyān. 前天.

1962. The day after tomorrow.
hòu-tyān. 後天.

1963. Two weeks ago.
lyǎng-ge lǐ-bài yǐ-chyán. 兩個礼拜以前.

WEATHER

1964. How is the weather today?
jīn-tyān de tyān-chì dzěm-ma-yàng?
今天的天氣怎麼樣?

1965. It looks like it's going to rain.
hǎu-syàng yàu syà-yǔ. 好像要下雨.

1966. It is [cold] [fair] [warm].
hěn [lěng] [shwáng-lǎng] [wēn nwǎn].
很 [冷] [爽朗] [溫暖].

1967. It is windy. fēng hěn dà. 風很大.

1968. The weather is clearing.
tyān-chì jèng jwǎn chíng. 天氣正轉晴.

1969. What a beautiful day!
tyān-chì hǎu jí le! 天氣好極了!

1970. I want to sit [in the shade].

wǒ yàu [dzài yīn-lyáng] dzwò syà.

我要[在陰涼]坐下.

1971. —in the sunshine.

—dzài tài-yáng gwāng. —在太陽光.

1972. —in a breeze.

—dzài wēi-fēng. —在微風.

1973. What is the weather forecast [for tomorrow]?

[míng-tyān de] tyān-chì yù bàu dzěm-ma-yàng?

[明天的]天氣預報怎麼樣?

1974. —for the weekend.

—jōu-mwò de. —週末的.

1975. It will snow tomorrow.

míng-tyān yàu syà sywě. 明天要下雪.

DAYS OF THE WEEK

1976. Sunday. syīng-chī-r̀. 星期日.

1977. Monday. syīng-chī-yī. 星期一.

1978. Tuesday. syīng-chī-èr. 星期二.

1979. Wednesday. syīng-chī-sān. 星期三

1980. Thursday. syīng-chī-sż. 星期四

1981. Friday. syīng-chī-wǔ. 星期五

1982. Saturday. syīng-chī-lyòu. 星期六.

DATES, MONTHS AND SEASONS

1983. January. jēng-ywè (OR: yī-ywè). 正月（一月）.

1984. February. èr-ywè. 二月.

1985. March. sān-ywè. 三月.

1986. April. sż-ywè. 四月.

1987. May. wǔ-ywè. 五月.

1988. June. lyòu-ywè. 六月.

1989. July. chī-ywè. 七月.

1990. August. bā-ywè. 八月.

1991. September. jyǒu-ywè. 九月.

1992. October. shŕ-ywè. 十月.

1993. November. shŕ-yí-ywè. 十一月.

1994. December. shŕ-èr-ywè. 十二月.

1995. The spring. chwūn-tyān. 春天.

1996. The summer. syà-tyān. 夏天.

1997. The autumn. chyōu-tyān. 秋天.

1998. The winter. dūng-tyān. 冬天.

1999. Today is the 31st of May, 1980.
jīn-tyān shŕ yì-jyǒu-bā-líng nyán wǔ-ywè sān-shŕ-yī-r̀.
今天是一九八〇年五月三十一日.

NUMBERS: CARDINALS

2000. Zero. líng. 零

2001. One. yī. 一.

2002. Two. èr.* 二

2003. Three. sān. 三

2004. Four. sż. 四

2005. Five. wǔ. 五

2006. Six. lyòu. 六

2007. Seven. chī. 七

2008. Eight. bā. 八

2009. Nine. jyǒu. 九

2010. Ten. shŕ. 十

2011. Eleven. shŕ-yī. 十一

2012. Twelve. shŕ-èr. 十二

2013. Thirteen. shŕ-sān. 十三

2014. Fourteen. shŕ-sż. 十四

2015. Fifteen. shŕ-wǔ. 十五

2016. Sixteen. shŕ-lyòu. 十六

2017. Seventeen. shŕ-chī. 十七

2018. Eighteen. shŕ-bā. 十八

2019. Nineteen. shŕ-jyǒu. 十九

2020. Twenty. èr-shŕ. 二十

2021. Twenty-one. èr-shŕ-yī. 二十一

2022. Twenty-five. èr-shŕ-wǔ. 二十五

2023. Thirty. sān-shŕ. 三十

2024. Forty. sż-shŕ. 四十

---

* In many grammatical situations, "two" is expressed by *lyǎng*(-*ge*).

2025. Fifty. wŭ-shŕ. 五十

2026. Sixty. lyòu-shŕ. 六十

2027. Seventy. chī-shŕ. 七十

2028. Eighty. bā-shŕ. 八十

2029. Ninety. jyŏu-shŕ. 九十

2030. One hundred. yì-băi. 一百

2031. One hundred and one.
yì-băi-líng-yī. 一百零一

2032. One hundred and ten.
yì-băi-yì-shŕ (OR: yì-băi-shŕ). 一百一十（一百十）

2033. One thousand. yī-chyān. 一千

2034. Two thousand. lyăng-chyān. 兩千

2035. Three thousand. sān-chyān. 三千

2036. Ten thousand.* yí-wàn. 一萬

2037. One hundred thousand.
shŕ-wàn. 十萬

2038. One million. yì-băi-wàn. 一百萬

NUMBERS: ORDINALS

2039. The first. dì-yī. 第一

2040. The second. dì-èr. 第二

2041. The third. dì-sān. 第三

2042. The fourth. dì-sż. 第四

---

* For numbers larger than 10,000 the Chinese count in terms of units of 10,000. Thus 205,100 is *èr-shŕ-wàn-líng-wŭ-chyān-yí-băi*.

043. The fifth. dì-wǔ. 第五.

044. The sixth. dì-lyòu. 第六.

045. The seventh. dì-chī. 第七.

046. The eighth. dì-bā. 第八.

047. The ninth. dì-jyǒu. 第九.

048. The tenth. dì-shŕ. 第十.

049. The twentieth. dì-èr-shŕ. 第二十.

050. The thirtieth. dì-sān-shŕ. 第三十.

051. The hundredth. dì-yì-bǎi. 第一百.

052. The thousandth. dì-yī-chyān. 第一千.

053. The ten thousandth. dì-yí-wàn. 第一萬.

QUANTITIES

054. A fraction. fēn-shù. 分數.

055. One quarter. sż-fēn-jř-yī. 四分之一.

056. One third. sān-fēn-jř-yī. 三分之一.

057. One half. yí-bàn. 一半.

058. Three quarters. sż-fēn-jř-sān. 四分之三.

059. The whole. chywán-bù. 全部.

060. A pair. yí-dwèi. 一對.

061. A dozen. yì-dá. 一打.

062. A few. yì-syē. 一些.

063. Several. jí-ge. 幾個.

064. Many. hěn-dwō. 很多.

FAMILY

2065. Wife. chī-dž. 妻子．

2066. Husband. jàng-fū. 丈夫．

2067. Mother. mǔ-chīn. 母親．

2068. Father. fù-chīn. 父親．

2069. Grandmother. dzú-mǔ. 祖母．

2070. Grandfather. dzǔ-fù. 祖父．

2071. Daughter. nyǔ-ér. 女兒．

2072. Son. ér-dz. 兒子．

2073. Granddaughter. swūn-nyǔ-ér. 孫女兒．

2074. Grandson. swūn-dz. 孫子．

2075. Older brother. gē-gē. 哥哥．

2076. Younger brother. dì-dì. 弟弟．

2077. Older sister. jyé-jyě. 姐姐．

2078. Younger sister. mèi-mèi. 妹妹．

2079. Aunt (wife of mother's brother).
jyòu-mǔ. 舅母．

2080. Aunt (mother's sister). yí-ma. 姨媽．

2081. Aunt (wife of father's elder brother).
bwó-mǔ. 伯母．

2082. Aunt (wife of father's younger brother).
shén-mǔ. 嬸母．

2083. Aunt (father's sister). gū-gū. 姑姑．

2084. Uncle (mother's brother).
jyòu-fù. 舅父．

2085. Uncle (husband of mother's sister).
yí-jàng. 姨丈.

2086. Uncle (father's elder brother).
bwó-bwó. 伯伯.

2087. Uncle (father's younger brother).
shú-shú. 叔叔.

2088. Uncle (husband of father's sister).
gū-jàng. 姑丈.

2089. Niece (brother's daughter).
jŕ-nyŭ. 侄女.

2090. Niece (sister's daughter).
wài-shēng-nyŭ. 外生女.

2091. Nephew (brother's son).
jŕ-ér. 侄兒.

2092. Nephew (sister's son).
wài-shēng. 外生.

2093. Older male cousin. byău-gē. 表哥.

2094. Younger male cousin. byău-dì. 表弟.

2095. Older female cousin.
byáu-jyĕ. 表姐.

2096. Younger female cousin.
byău-mèi. 表妹.

2097. Father-in-law. ywè-fù. 岳父.

2098. Mother-in-law. ywè-mŭ. 岳母.

2099. Relative. chīn-chī. 親戚.

2100. Adults. dà-rén. 大人.

2101. Children. hái-dz. 孩子.

COMMON SIGNS AND PUBLIC NOTICES

2102. Admission. rù-cháng. 入場.

2103. Admission free.
myǎn-fèi rù-cháng. 免費入場.

2104. Air conditioned.
gūng chì tyǎu jyě. 空氣調解.

2105. Attention. jù-yì. 注意.

2106. Bargain. táu jyà. 投價.

2107. Beware of dog.
jǐn-fáng gǒu yǎu. 謹防狗咬.

2108. Bus stop.
(gūng-gùng chì)-chē-jàn. (公共汽) 車站.

2109. Business school.
shāng-yè sywé-syàu. 商業學校

2110. Cemetery. fén-di. 墳地.

2111. City hall. shr̀-jèng-fǔ-li tīng. 市政府.

2112. Clinic. jēn-lyáu-swǒ. 診療所.

2113. (Closed for) vacation.
syōu-jyà. 休假.

2114. Closed [from 8 A.M. to 9 P.M.].
[tsúng wǎn-shàng bā-dyǎn dàu dzǎu-shàng jyóu-dyǎn
bù-kāi-mén.
[從晚上八點到早上九點.] 不開門.

2115. Closed on Sundays and holidays.
syīng-chī-r̀ hé jyà-r̀ bù-kāi-mén. 星期日和假日不開門

2116. Cold. lěng. 冷.

2117. Continuous performance.
yán-syù yǎn-dzòu. 連續演奏.

2118. Danger. wēi-syǎn. 危險.

2119. Departure. chǐ-chéng. 恣程.

2120. Diner. syǎu tsān-gwǎn. 小餐館.

2121. Dining car. tsān chē. 餐車.

2122. Dining room. tsān shr̀. 餐室.

2123. Do not feed the animals.
bù yàu wèi dùng-wù. 不要餵動物.

2124. Down. syà. 下.

2125. Emergency exit.
tài-píng mén. 太平門.

2126. Employees only (OR: **No admittance to un-
authorized persons**).
dž ywán jywàn yùng. 職員專用.

2127. Enter. jìn rù. 進入.

2128. Entrance. rù kǒu. 入口.

2129. Exit. chū kǒu. 出口.

2130. Forbidden. jìn-jř. 禁止.

2131. For sale. chū-shòu. 出售.

2132. Free. myǎn-fèi de. 免費的.

2133. Furnished rooms for rent.
bèi yǒu jyā-jyù de fáng-jyān chū dzū.
備有家具的房間出租.

2134. Men's room. nán-tsè-swǒ. 男劇所.

2135. Hospital. yī-ywàn. 医院.

2136. Hot. rè. 熱.

2137. House for rent.
fáng-wū chū dzū.　房屋出租.

2138. Information (desk).
wèn-syùn-chù.　問詢處.

2139. Janitor. gwǎn-lǐ-rén.　管理人.

2140. Keep off the grass.
wù tà tsǎu-dì.　勿踏草地.

2141. Ladies' room. nyǔ-tsè-swǒ.　女厠所.

2142. Library. tú-shū-gwǎn.　圖書館

2143. Men at work.
yǒu rén dzài gūng-dzwò.　有人在工作.

2144. No noise.
chǐng wù chǎu-nàu (OR: ān-jìng).　請勿嘈鬧 (安靜).

2145. No performance.
syōu-syϊ.　休息.

2146. No smoking. jìn yān.　禁煙.

2147. No spitting. jìn-jǐ tù-tán.　禁止吐痰.

2148. No swimming.
bù syǔ yóu-yǔng.　不許游泳.

2149. No trespassing.
bù syǔ shàn-rù.　不許擅入.

2150. Notices. tūng-jϊ.　通知.

2151. Occupied. yǒu rén dzài nèi.　有人在內.

2152. On sale here. chū shòu chù.　出售處.

2153. [Open] from 9 A.M. to 8 P.M.
tsúng dzǎu-shàng jyóu-dyǎn [kāi] dàu wǎn-shàng bā-dyǎn
從早上九點 [開] 到晚上八點.

2154. Pedestrians only.
syíng rén jwān yùng.　行人專用.

2155. Post no bills. jìn-jǐ jāu-tyē. 禁止招貼.

2156. Private property.
sž-yǒu tsái-chǎn. 私有財産.

2157. Private road. sž-rén lù. 私人路.

2158. Pull. lā. 拉.

2159. Push. twēi. 推.

2160. Railroad station.
hwǒ-chē-jàn. 火車站.

2161. Refreshments. yǐn-shŕ-pǐn. 飲食品.

2162. Refuse. là sè. 拉圾.

2163. Reserved. dìng dzwò. 定坐.

2164. Retail. líng-shòu de. 零售的.

2165. Ring the bell.
chǐng àn mén-líng. 請摸門鈴.

2166. Self-service. dž-jǐ ná. 自己拿.

2167. Silence (OR: **Quiet**).
ān-jìng. 安靜.

2168. Smoking car. syī-yān chē. 吸煙車.

2169. Smoking forbidden.
jìn-jǐ syī-yān. 禁止吸煙.

2170. Stairs. lóu-tī. 樓梯.

2171. To the trains.
syàng hwǒ-chē. 向火車.

2172. Toilet. tsè-swǒ. 厠所.

2173. Up. shàng. 上.

2174. Vacant. kūng de. 空的.

2175. Warning. jǐng-gàu. 警告.

2176. Watch your step.
syău-syīn jyău-bù.　小心脚步.

2177. Wet paint.　yóu-chī wèi-gān. 油漆未乾.

2178. Wholesale.　pī-fā de. 批發的.

2179. Will return at [1 P.M.].
[syà-wǔ yì-dyǎn] hwéi lái. [下午一點] 回來.

2180. Zoo.　dùng-wù-ywán. 動物園.

INDEX

Words in this book are indexed by phrase numbers (1–2180), but section headings (capitalized) and subheadings (in small capitals) are indexed by page numbers. Parts of speech are indicated (where there might be confusion) by abbreviations: *adj.* for adjective, *adv.* for adverb, *n.* for noun, *prep.* for preposition, *v.* for verb. Parentheses contain explanations.

Because of the large amount of material, cross-indexing has not been feasible. Common expressions of two or more words will be found under only one of their components, e.g. "good afternoon" is under "good," not "afternoon." If you do not find an expression under one of its words, try another. Where a numbered sentence contains a choice of Chinese equivalents, only the first one has been indexed.

Every English entry is followed by its Chinese equivalent in transcription. If you wish to see the characters as well, refer back to the original sentence. Look at all the sentences listed for a particular word to become familiar with the different shades of meaning of the various Chinese equivalents.

cabbage: *yáng-bái-tsài* 917;
  Chinese —: *bái-tsài* 918
cabin (of ship): *kè-tsāng* 235;
  — steward: *chwán-chāng*
  fú wù shēng 240
cablegram: *hǎi-wài-dyàn-*
  bàu 508
CAFÉ AND BAR, p. 51
cake: *gāu dyán* 1006
calf (of leg): *syáu-twěi* 1883
call (n.): *dyàn-hwà* 516;
  (v.): *jǎu* 514; *dǎ* 535;
  (summon): *jyàu* 172; —
  for: *lái-jyē* 1114
camera: *jàu-syàng-jī* 1563
CAMERA SHOP AND
  PHOTOGRAPHY, p.
  105
camping: *lù-yíng* 1254
campsite: *lù-yíng dì* 1253
can (aux. v.): *ké-yi* 124;
  néng 570
cancel: *chyǔ-syāu* 242
candle: *là-jú* 629
candy: *táng-dz* 1007; *táng-*
  gwǒ 1580
cane: *shǒu-jàng* 1369
canned: *gwàn-tóu de* 740
can opener: *kāi-gwàn-chì*
  653
cantaloupe: *tyán-gwā* 974
Canton: *gwǎng-dūng* 1066
cap: *syáu-màu* 1370
captain: *chwán-jǎng* 238
car: *chē* 333; *chì-chē* 370

carbon paper: *fù-syé jř* 1470
carburetor: *tàn-hwà-chì* 410
cards (playing): *jř-pái* 1228
careful: *syáu-syīn* 34
carefully: *syáu-syīn de* 175
carp: *lǐ-yú* 879
carriage (baby): *yīng-hái*
  chē 1745
carrot: *húng-lwó-bwō* 919
carry: *ná-dàu* 168; *ná* 170;
  dài 259
cash (v.): *hwàn syàn-kwǎn*
  1273
cashew: *yāu-gwǒ* 975
cashier: *chū-nà-ywán* 614
cashier's desk: *chū-nà-chù*
  787
castle: *chéng-bǎu* 1133
cathedral: *dà jyàu-táng* 1127
Catholic: *tyān-jǔ* 1154
cauliflower: *yáng-tsài-hwār*
  920
cave: *dùng sywè* 1129
cavity: *jù-chř* 1854
celery: *chín-tsài* 921
cemetery: *fén-di* 2110
center of town: *shř-jūng-syīn*
  183
ceramics: *táu chì* 1445
cereal: *mài-pyàn* 835
certificate: *jèng-shū* 146
chair: *yǐ-dz* 654
CHAMBERMAID, p. 47
chambermaid: *nyǔ-shř-jě*
  593

champagne: *syāng-bīng jyǒu* 705

change (n.): *líng chyán* 329; (v.): *hwàn* 309; *hwàn-hwàn* 381

charge (n.): *dài-jyà* 510; *chyán* 790; *fèi-yùng* 1215; *fèi* 1356

chassis: *chē-pán* 411

cheap: *pyán-yì* 1297

cheaper: *gèng pyán-yì* 577

check (n.): *jī-pyàu* 1273; traveler's —: *lyǔ-syíng jī-pyàu* 1274; (bill): *jàng-dān* 786

check (v.): *chá* 159; (baggage): *twō yùn* 160; — in (at airport): *dēng-jì* 248

checkers: *chí* 1234

checkroom: *yī màu jì fàng chù* 1676

cheek: *sāi-jyá* 1884

cherry: *yīng-táu* 976

chess: *syàng chí* 1233

chest (body): *syūng* 1885

chestnut: *lì-dz* 977

chest of drawers: *yī-gwèi* 655

chewing gum: *kǒu syāng* 1499

chic: *syáu-sǎ* 1304

chicken: *jī* 774; drunken —: *jyǒu-jī* 1021; boneless —: *rwǎn-jī* 1023

chicken pox: *shwěi-dòu* 1809

children: *hái-dz* 2101

children's clothes: *túng-jwāng* 1371

children's clothing store: *syǎu-hái-dz bù dyàn* 1678

chili paste: *là jyàng* 795

chili peppers: *là-jyāu* 805

chill (n.): *fā lěng* 1810

chin: *syà-bā-gù kē-er* 1886

china: *tsź-chì* 1446

Chinese (language): *jūng-gwo hwà* 118; (adj.): *jūng-gwo* 180

CHINESE FOOD, p. 70

CHINESE LIQUORS, p. 76

chocolate: *chyǎu-kè-lì* 1011; hot —: *rè de chyǎu-kè-lì yǐn-lyàu* 823

choke (n.): *bì-sè-bù* 412

chop (cut of meat): *pái-gǔ ròu* 856

chopped: *chyē-syì de* 755

chopsticks: *kwài-dz* 730

choral music: *jàn-měi-shī* 1155

Christmas: *shèng-dàn* 1099

church: *jyàu-táng* 1154

cigar: *syāng yān* 1594; — store: *syāng yān dyàn* 1593

cigarette: *yān* 1595

CIGAR STORE, p. 107

cinnamon: *gwèi-pí* 796

circus: *mǎ-syì chǎng* 1195

citizen: *gūng-mín* 85

hundred (one): *yì-bǎi* 2030;
— and one: *yì-bǎi-líng-yī*
2031; — and ten: *yì-bǎi-yì-shŕ* 2032

hundredth: *dì-yì-bǎi* 2051

hungry, be: *jywé-de è* 98

hurry, be in a: *gǎn shŕ-jyān* 325

hurt (*v.*): *tùng* 1852

husband: *syān-shēng* 1867; *jàng-fū* 2066

I: *wǒ* 39

ice (cubes): *bīng-kwài* 598;
— bag: *bīng dài* 1526;
— cream: *bīng-jī-líng* 1011

iced: *bīng* 825

ice skating, go: *hwá bīng* 1248

identification: *shēn-fèn-jèng* 1349; — card: *shēn-fèn-jèng* 145

ignition: *chǐ-dùng* 441

imitation: *fǎng dzàu pǐn* 1334

immediately: *gǎn-kwài* 1481

in: *dzài* 155; (with respect to): *dwèi* 1119; (inside): *nèi* 377; (to): *chéng* 1654; *lǐ* 1762; (within a period of time): *yǐ-hòu* 328

include: *bāu-gwà* 337; *jyā shàng* 574; *bāu-kwò* 788

indigestion: *syāu-hwà bù lyáng* 1826

indoors: *lǐ-tóu* 719

inexpensive: *pyán-yì* 540

infection: *chwán-rǎn* 1827

inflammation: *húng jǔng* 1828

influenza: *gǎn-màu* 1829

information office (or desk): *wèn-syùn-chù* 292

injection: *jù-shè* 1782

ink: *mwò-shwěi* 1463

inner tube: *nèi-tāi* 442

insect: *kwūn-chúng* 622; *chúng* 1804

insecticide: *shā chúng yàu* 1527

inside: *lǐ-tóu* 203; *syàng nèi* 555

insomnia: *shŕ-mín jèng* 1830

instrument panel: *yí-chì-bǎn* 443

insurance policy: *báu-syǎn-gūng-sż* 338

insure: *báu-syǎn* 499

interested, be: *yǒu syìng-chyù* 1119

interesting: *yǒu syìng-chyù* 1115; *yǒu yì-sż* 1142

intermission: *jūng-jyān syōu-syì* 1190

internally: *nèi* 1488

international: *gwó-jì* 334

intersection: *shŕ-dż lù-kǒu* 364

puppet: *gwĕi-lĕi* 1207
purple: *dž sè* 1425
purser: *chwán-shàng de shì-wù jăng* 239
push: *twēi* 372
put: *fàng* 384

QUANTITIES, p. 135
quarter (one): *sż-fēn-jř-yī* 2055; three quarters: *sż-fēn-jř-sān* 2058
quarter (past): *yí-kè* 1941
quickly: *kwài dyăr* 724
quiet: *ān-jìng* 543

rabbi: *yóu-tài jyàu shén-fu* 1166
radiator (car): *shwĕi-syāng* 384; *lĕng-chywè-chì* 460
radio: *wú-syàn-dyàn* 461
radish: *húng-syí-lwó-bwō* 941
rag: *mwó-bù* 462
railroad station: *hwŏ-chē-jàn* 295
rain (v.): *syà-yŭ* 1965
raincoat: *yŭ-yī* 1394
raisin: *pú-táu-kān* 1001
rare (meat): *hĕn nwùn de* 769
rate: *jyà-gé* 335; *hwèi-lyù* 1271
rattle: *yău-gú* 1754
razor (electric): *dyàn tì dāu* 1540; (safety): *ān-chywán tì dāu* 1540; (straight):

jŕ tì dāu 1540; — blade: *tì dāu pyàn* 1541
reach (arrive at): *dàu-dá* 511
read: *nyàn* 105
ready (adj.): *hău* 1337; (v.): *jéng-lĭ* 593
real estate office: *dì-chăn gūng-shř* 1716
rear (prep.): *bèi-hòu* 210
reasonable (in price): *jyà-chyán gūng-dàu* 1298
receipt: *shōu-tyáu* 500
receptacle: *tŭng* 1260
recharge: *chūng-dyàn* 385
recommend: *jyè-shàu* 710
red: *húng* 707; *húng sè* 1426
reference: *bău-jèng-rén* 1350
refreshments: *yĭn-shŕ-pĭn* 2161
refund: *fù hwán* 1358
refuse (n.): *là sè* 2162
regards: *wèn-hou* 54
registration desk: *dēng-jì-chù* 546
registration form: *dēng-jì-byău* 547
regular: *píng-cháng* 379
relative: (n.): *chīn-chī* 2099
reliable: *kàu de jù* 1735
relieve: *jŕ* 1769
remedy: *yàu* 229; *jŕ-lyáu* 1795
remember: *jì-de* 133

socks: *dwǎn wā* 1406

soda: *sū-dǎ shwěi* 690

soft-boiled: *bàn-shú de* 838

softer: *gèng róu-rwǎn* 1305

sole (fish): *tǎ-yú* 902; (shoe): *syé-dǐ* 1620

some: *yi-syē* 598

someone: *yǒu-rén* 346

something else: *chí-tā de* 777

son: *ér-dz* 2072

soon: *gǎn-kwài* 613

sore, be: *tùng* 1852

sore throat: *hóu-tóu fá-yán* 1839

sorry, be: *dwèi-bu-chǐ* 20

soup: *tāng* 844; — spoon: *tāng-chí* 736

SOUPS, p. 71

SOUPS AND SALADS, p. 61

sour: *swān* 1036

south: *nán* 185

souvenir: *jì-nyàn pǐn* 1591

soybean curd: *dòu-fú* 945

soybeans: *hwáng-dòu* 944

soy sauce: *jyáng-yóu* 814

spareribs: *pái-gǔ* 1022

spare tire: *yù-bèi-lwún-tāi* 475

spark plugs: *hwǒ sè* 469

speak: *shwō* 102; *jyáng* 103; *jyǎng-hwà* 123

special delivery: *tè-byé jwān-sùng* 493

specialist: *jwān-jyā* 1796

specialty of the house: *běn gwǎr de té-byè tsài* 722

speedometer: *sù-dù-jì* 470

spell (v.): *pīn* 119

spicy: *jyā yǒu syāng lyàu de* 747

spinach: *bwō-tsài* 946

spine: *jí-gǔ* 1925

spitting: *tù-án* 2147

spleen: *pí* 1926

sponge: *hǎi myán* 1552

sporting goods: *yùn-dùng yùng-jyù* 1724

SPORTS AND GAMES, p. 86

sports event: *yùn-dùng bǐ-sài* 1209

sprain (n.): *nyǒu-shāng* 1838

spray (n.): *jì* 622

spring (metal): *tán-hwáng* 471; (season): *chwūn-tyān* 1995; — festival: *chwūn-jyè* 1104

spring roll: *chwūn-jywǎn* 1016

squab: *rǔ-gē* 875

square (n., plaza): *gwǎng-chǎng* 204

squash: *gwā* 947

squid: *yǒu-yú* 903

stage: *tái-shàng* 1185

stain: *dzāng-r* 1608

stairs: *lóu-tī* 213

stale: *bu syīn-syan* 765

stamp (n.): *yóu-pyàu* 502

time: *shŕ-jyān* 281; (free):
kùng-r 1152; at what —:
shém-ma shŕ-hòu 226; *jĭ-dyán jūng* 243; what —
is it: *shém-ma shŕ-hòu le* 1937

time, on: *jwŭn-shŕ* 79

timetable: *shŕ-jyān byáu* 279

tip (n.), *shǎng-chyán* 177;
syáu-fèi 788; (v.): *gěi syáu-fèi* 1188

tire: *chē-tāi* 375; *chē-lwún* 388; *lwún-tāi* 389; —
pump: *dǎ-chì-tŭng* 477

tired: *lèi* 99

to: *syàng* 54; *dàu* 96; *wàng* 243

toast: *kǎu myàn-bāu* 832

tobacco: *yān-tsǎu* 1603

today: *jīn-tyān* 501

toe: *jyǎu-jĭ-tóu* 1764

together: *yi-chĭ* 1629

toilet: *tsé-swǒ* 618; — paper
tsǎu-jĭ 635

token: *dài yùng hwò bèi* 312

tomato: *fān-chyé* 828

tomb: *mù-líng* 1137

tomorrow: *míng-tyān* 1114

tongue: *shé-tóu* 868

tonic (beverage): *jīn-jī-nà shwěi* 694

tonight: *jīn-tyān wǎn-shàng* 545

tonsillitis: *byǎn-táu-syàn yán* 1843

tonsils: *byǎn-táu-syàn* 1933

too (much): *tài* 585

tools: *gūng-jyù* 478

tooth: *yá-chǐ* 1851; *chǐ* 1853

toothache: *yá tùng* 1844

toothbrush: *yá-shwā* 1557

toothpaste: *yá-gāu* 1558

toothpowder: *yá-fěn* 1559

top: *shàng-tóu* 214; *shàng bù* 1639

torn, be: *sž-pwò le* 1617

tough: *yìng* 766

tourist office: *lyǔ-syíng shè* 180

tourist trap: *pyàn yŏu-kè de dì-fāng* 1140

tourniquet: *jí-sywě dài* 1868

towel: *máu-jīn* 636

town: *shŕ* 353

toy: *wán-jyù* 1592

track: *tái* 278

traffic: *jyāu-tūng* 359; —
circle: *ywán hwán* 215;
— light: *jyāu-tūng dēng* 199

TRAIN, p. 22

train: *hwǒ-chē* 131

tranquilizer: *jèn-jìng jì* 1485

transfer (n.): *hwàn chē pyàu* 311; (v.): *hwàn chē* 309

transmission (automatic):
dž-dùng-byàn-sù 479;
(standard): *shǒu-byàn-sù* 480

LISTEN & LEARN CASSETTES

Complete, practical at-home language learning courses for people with limited study time—specially designed for travelers.

Special features:

* Dual-language—Each phrase first in English, then the foreign-language equivalent, followed by a pause for repetition (allows for easy use of cassette even without manual).

* Native speakers—Spoken by natives of the country who are language teachers at leading colleges and universities.

* Convenient manual—Contains every word on the cassettes—all fully indexed for fast phrase or word location.

Each boxed set contains one 90-minute cassette and complete manual.

Listen & Learn French .... Cassette and Manual
99914-9 $8.95

Listen & Learn German .... Cassette and Manual
99915-7 $8.95

Listen & Learn Italian .... Cassette and Manual
99916-5 $8.95

Listen & Learn Japanese .... Cassette and Manual
99917-3 $8.95

Listen & Learn Modern Greek .... Cassette and Manual
99921-1 $8.95

Listen & Learn Modern Hebrew .... Cassette and Manual
99923-8 $8.95

Listen & Learn Portuguese .... Cassette and Manual
99919-X $8.95

Listen & Learn Russian .... Cassette and Manual
99920-3 $8.95

Listen & Learn Spanish .... Cassette and Manual
99918-1 $8.95

Listen & Learn Swedish .... Cassette and Manual
99922-X $8.95

Precise, to-the-point guides for adults with limited learning time

ESSENTIAL GRAMMAR SERIES

Designed for independent study or as supplements to conventional courses, the *Essential Grammar* series provides clear explanations of all aspects of grammar—no trivia, no archaic material. Do not confuse these volumes with abridged grammars. These volumes are complete.

ESSENTIAL FRENCH GRAMMAR, Seymour Resnick. Includes 2500 item cognate list. 159pp. 5¾ × 8¼.

•20419-7 Pa. $2.75

ESSENTIAL GERMAN GRAMMAR, Guy Stern and E. F. Bleiler. Unusual shortcuts on noun declension, word order. 124pp. 5¾ × 8¼.

•20422-7 Pa. $2.95

ESSENTIAL ITALIAN GRAMMAR, Olga Ragusa. Includes useful discussion of verb idioms essential in Italian. 111pp. 5¾ × 8¼.

•20779-X Pa. $2.95

ESSENTIAL JAPANESE GRAMMAR, E. F. Bleiler. In Romaji, no characters needed. Japanese grammar is regular and simple. 156pp. 5¾ × 8¼.

21027-8 Pa. $2.95

ESSENTIAL PORTUGUESE GRAMMAR, Alexander da R. Prista. Includes 4 appendices covering regular, irregular verbs. 114pp. 5¾ × 8¼.

21650-0 Pa. $3.50

ESSENTIAL SPANISH GRAMMAR, Seymour Resnick. Includes 2500 word cognate list. 115pp. 5¾ × 8¼.

•20780-3 Pa. $2.75

ESSENTIAL ENGLISH GRAMMAR, Philip Gucker. Combines modern functional and traditional approaches. 177pp. 8¼.

21649-7 Pa. $3.50

available in British Commonwealth Countries except da.